Shining Star A

Workbook

Anna Uhl Chamot

Pam Hartmann

Jann Huizenga

with

Steve Sloan

Longman

longman.com

Shining Star ★ A

Workbook

Pearson Education, 10 Bank Street, White Plains, NY 10606

Workbook consultant: Steve Sloan

Vice president, director of instructional design: Allen Ascher
Editorial director: Ed Lamprich
Acquisitions editor: Amanda Rappaport Dobbins
Project manager: Susan Saslow
Workbook manager: Donna Schaffer
Senior development editor: Virginia Bernard
Vice president, director of design and production: Rhea Banker
Executive managing editor: Linda Moser
Production manager: Ray Keating
Senior production editor: Sylvia Dare
Director of manufacturing: Patrice Fraccio
Senior manufacturing buyer: Edith Pullman
Photo research: Kirchoff/Wohlberg, Inc.
Design and production: Kirchoff/Wohlberg, Inc.
Cover design: Rhea Banker, Tara Mayer
Text font: 11/14 Franklin Gothic
Acknowledgments: See page 169
Illustrations: 10 Barry Rockwell; 17 Andrea Wesson; 45 Dom Lee;
    70 Phil Scheuer; 73 Jeffrey Lindberg; 82 Liz Callen; 101 John Hovell;
    158 Lee MacLeod.
Photos: 3, 13, 26, 27 Dorling Kindersley; 60 Roger Wood/CORBIS;
    66 Bettmann/CORBIS; 67 Stone/Getty Images; 68 Adam Woolfitt/CORBIS;
    81 Dorling Kindersley; 96 Stuart Franklin/Magnum Photos; 112 Alexandra
    Boulat/SIPA Press; 115 Jim Zuckerman/CORBIS; 122 Erich Lessing/Art
    Resource; 122 CORBIS; 124 Mansell/Timepix; 130 Hulton/Archive/Getty
    Images; 138 Hulton/Archive/Getty Images; 140 Dorling Kindersley;
    150 Detlev van Ravenswaay/Photo Researchers; 152 AFP/CORBIS;
    157 Digital Art/CORBIS; 164 Department of Electrical & Electronic
    Engineering, University of Portsmouth, England; 165 AP/Wide World Photos;
    166 Digital Art/CORBIS; 168 NASA.

ISBN: 0-13-049954-4

Printed in the United States of America
    12 13 14 15 16-BAH-12 11 10 09 08

Welcome to *Shining Star's* Workbook. Exercises in each unit of this book will help you practice the skills and strategies you've already learned throughout the *Shining Star* program. You'll have fun completing crossword puzzles as you build your vocabulary. Other activities will help you apply reading strategies and practice language-development skills in grammar, spelling, writing, proofreading, and editing.

To help you get the most out of your *Shining Star* reading experiences, we've added an exciting feature—Reader's Companion. The Reader's Companion activities will help you better understand and explore the "Connect to Literature" and "Connect to Content" selections in your Student Book.

Reader's Companion begins with a summary that tells you what the selection is about before you read. Then a visual summary helps you focus on the main ideas and details, as well as the organization of each selection. Use What You Know lets you explore your own knowledge or experience before you read. You'll apply reading strategies that you've already learned and show that you know about the kind of selection you're reading—whether it's an informational text or a song. You'll check your comprehension or understanding of a selection and enjoy using literary elements. You'll find write-on-lines for recording your answers. Whenever you see the Mark the Text symbol, you'll know that you should underline, circle, or mark the text. We hope you enjoy choosing from the many creative activities designed to suit your own learning styles.

After reading, Reader's Companion will give you opportunities to retell selections in creative ways—using your own words. You can also write your thoughts and reactions to the selection. Then you can comment on how certain skills and strategies were helpful to you. Thinking about a skill will help you apply it to other reading situations.

We hope you'll enjoy showing what you know as you complete the many and varied activities included in your *Shining Star* Workbook.

CONTENTS

CONTENTS

CONTENTS

UNIT 1 Growing Up
PART 1

Contents

VOCABULARY

Use with textbook page 5.

Complete each sentence. Use the words in the box. You will use each word once.

citizen	cultures	education	rights

1. In some _____, children learn at home.

2. Learning to write is an important part of a good _____.

3. A good _____ follows the law and respects the community.

4. When everyone is treated fairly, people have equal _____.

Read the clues below the crossword puzzle. Then use the words in the box to complete the crossword puzzle. (Hint: You will not use all the words.)

ancient	formal	citizen	poetry	education
festivals	ceremony	literature	cultures	rights

ACROSS
  3. schooling
  5. things the law says you can have or do; freedoms
  6. groups of people's customs, way of life, and traditions

DOWN
  1. formal event to mark a special occasion; ritual
  2. very old
  4. person who belongs to a country

VOCABULARY BUILDING

Compound Words

Draw a line from a word in list A to a word in list B to make a **compound word**. Notice that when combined, these words make one new word. There is no space between the words. Some other compound words have a space between them, such as "pull toy."

Example: | child + hood = childhood |

List A	List B
1. school	horse
2. new	father
3. grand	snake
4. house	thing
5. knuckle	selves
6. rattle	born
7. after	bones
8. every	life
9. them	books
10. hobby	hold

READING STRATEGY

Use with textbook page 5.

Previewing

Previewing is looking at a text before you read it. You can preview a text to find out what it is about. When you read an informational text, use these parts of the text to help you preview:

- Title: the name of the text
- Subtitles: the titles for each part of the selection
- Art and captions: the drawings, photographs, and graphs, and the captions, or words, that describe them

1. Look at the informational text on pages 6–11 in your textbook. Write the title and subtitles.

   Title: _____

   Subtitles: _____

   _____

   _____

Now, look at the drawings, photos, and timelines on pages 6–11 in your textbook. Complete these sentences.

2. The picture on page 6 shows _____

   _____.

3. The picture at the top of page 8 shows _____

   _____.

4. The pictures on page 9 show_____

   _____.

5. Look at the timeline on page 10 in your textbook. The Maya civilization

   lasted_____

   _____

   _____

Use with textbook pages 14–16.

Summary: "Aesop's The Hare and the Tortoise"

In "The Hare and the Tortoise," the slow Tortoise challenges the speedy Hare to a race. Tortoise shows that "slow and steady wins the race."

Visual Summary

Main Characters
Hare, Tortoise

Conflict		
Hare thinks he can win because he is so fast and Tortoise is so slow.	← →	Tortoise thinks she can win. Hare is fast, but she is steady.

Solution (Outcome)
Tortoise plods on. The overconfident Hare takes a nap. Tortoise, the slow and steady one, plods on and wins the race.

Summary: "Why Rattlesnake Has Fangs"

The story "Why Rattlesnake Has Fangs" tells how the helpless Rattlesnake found a way to protect himself.

Visual Summary

What the Myth Explains
How the rattlesnake got his fangs

Problem
Rattlesnake had a rattle to warn others but no way to protect himself.

Solution
The Sun God felt sorry for him. He told Rattlesnake to get two sharp thorns from the devil's claw plant and put them in his mouth. Then Rattlesnake could warn other animals and protect himself with his fangs.

Aesop's The Hare and the Tortoise

On a hot, sunny day, Hare saw Tortoise **plodding** along on the road. Hare **teased** Tortoise because she was walking so slowly.

Tortoise laughed. "You can tease me if you like, but I bet I can get to the end of the field before you can. Do you want to race?"

Hare agreed, thinking he could easily win. He ran off. Tortoise plodded **steadily** after him.

Before long, Hare began to feel hot and tired. "I'll take a short **nap**," he thought. "If Tortoise passes me, I can **catch up to** her." Hare lay down and fell asleep.

Tortoise plodded on steadily, one foot after another.

The day was hot. Hare slept and slept in the heat. He slept for a longer time than he wanted. And Tortoise plodded on, slowly and steadily.

---

plodding, walking slowly
teased, made fun of, laughed at
steadily, at the same speed
nap, a short sleep
catch up to, go faster and pass

Choose one and complete it.
1. Draw a picture of the race.
2. Do research about foot races. List your notes.
3. Read what Tortoise said to Hare. What do you think Hare said when he agreed? Write his response. How would you say what each character said? What tone of voice would you use? List some ideas.

Finally, Hare woke up. He had slept longer than he wanted, but he still felt **confident** that he could reach the **finish line** before Tortoise.

He looked around. Tortoise was nowhere in sight. "Ha! Tortoise isn't even here yet!" he thought.

Hare started to run again. He leaped easily over roots and rocks. As he ran around the last corner and stopped to rest, he was amazed to see Tortoise still plodding steadily on, one foot after another, nearer and nearer the finish line.

Now Hare ran as fast as he could. He almost flew! But it was too late. He threw himself over the finish line, but Tortoise was there first.

"So what do you say?" asked Tortoise. But Hare was too tired to answer.

MORAL: Slow and steady wins the race.

---

confident, sure, certain
finish line, end of the race

Choose one and complete it.
1. Draw a picture of Hare and Tortoise at the end of the race.
2. Do research about hares or tortoises. Take notes.
3. How would you act out what happened at the finish line? Write some ideas.

Literary Element: Personification

Remember that personification is giving human traits to animals or things. Underline an example of personification. What trait made Hare lose? What trait made Tortoise win?

_____
_____
_____
_____
_____

Comprehension Check

Underline the question Tortoise asks Hare. What do you think Tortoise expected Hare to answer?

_____
_____
_____
_____
_____

Text Structure: Fable

Find the moral. Rewrite it in your own words.

_____
_____
_____
_____

Use What You Know

List three things used to warn others about something dangerous.

1. _____

2. _____

3. _____

Text Structure: Myth

This myth explains how the rattlesnake got his fangs. As you read, think about the explanation. Do you think this is really how rattlesnakes got fangs? Why?

_____

_____

_____

Reading Strategy: Compare and Contrast

As you read, notice the adjectives used to describe Rattlesnake. Underline them. What comparisons can you make about Rattlesnake before and after he got his fangs?

MARK THE TEXT

_____

_____

_____

Literary Element: Personification

List two things Rattlesnake does that an animal in real life cannot do.

1. _____

2. _____

Why Rattlesnake Has Fangs
by Cheryl Giff

Rattlesnake used to be the gentlest little animal. The Sun God forgot to give Rattlesnake a **weapon** to protect himself, and he was called the Soft Child.

The animals liked to hear him rattle, so they teased him all the time. One day at a ceremonial dance, a mean little rabbit said, "Let's have some fun with Soft Child."

He started to throw helpless little Rattlesnake around.

"Catch," yelled Skunk as he threw Soft Child back to Rabbit.

They had a good time, but Rattlesnake was unhappy and there was nothing he could do about it.

The Sun God felt sorry for the sad little snake, and he told him what to do.

"Get two sharp **thorns** from the devil's claw plant and put them in your mouth."

Rattlesnake picked the devil's claw and put the thorns in his upper jaw.

"Now you will have to rattle to give a **warning**," the Sun God told him. "**Strike** only if you have to."

The next day, Rabbit started to kick the snake and throw him around the way he always did.

Rattlesnake began to rattle his warning, but Rabbit just laughed and kicked him again. Soft Child remembered the thorns he held in his mouth. He used them on Rabbit.

After that, every animal backed away from Rattlesnake, and he was not called Soft Child any longer.

To this day, Rattlesnake strikes only if he has to, but everyone fears him.

---

fangs, big, sharp teeth
weapon, something you use to fight with
thorns, sharp spikes on a plant

warning, sign that something bad will happen
strike, hit

Retell It!

Choose one:
- Retell the fable from Hare's point of view.
- Retell the myth from Rattlesnake's point of view.

Take notes on the lines below to help you.

_____

_____

_____

_____

Reader's Response

Are you more like Hare or Tortoise? Tell why.

_____

_____

Would you have done what Sun God did to help Rattlesnake? Tell why.

_____

_____

_____

Think About the Skill

What predictions did you make about Hare and Tortoise? How did making predictions help you understand the fable better?

_____

_____

_____

What comparisons did you make about Rattlesnake at the beginning and at the end of the myth? How did making these comparisons help you understand the myth better?

_____

_____

_____

_____

GRAMMAR

Use with textbook page 18.

Using Adjectives to Describe

Adjectives are words used to describe nouns. Nouns are words for people, places, and things.

Adjectives can come after the verb.

> **verb adjective**
> The snake is sad.

Adjectives can also come before the noun.

> **adjective noun**
> The snake has a sad frown.
>
> **adjective noun**
> The helpless snake cries.

Do not add -s to an adjective when it describes a plural noun.

> I see the smart animals.

Draw a line under the adjective in each sentence. Then look at the position of the adjective. Does it come after the verb or before the noun? Circle the answer.

1. The hare is lazy.

    after the verb   before the noun

2. The slow tortoise wins the race.

    after the verb   before the noun

3. Snakes can be dangerous.

    after the verb   before the noun

4. Rattlesnakes are noisy.

    after the verb   before the noun

5. Ancient fables often teach lessons.

    after the verb   before the noun

6. Fables are funny.

    after the verb   before the noun

7. School in Rome was expensive.

    after the verb   before the noun

8. The lyre was popular in Greece.

    after the verb   before the noun

9. We will visit the ancient city.

    after the verb   before the noun

10. In Greece, girls played with terra-cotta dolls.

    after the verb   before the noun

GRAMMAR

Use after the lesson about the present tense.

Present Tense: Regular and Irregular Verbs
Some verbs are **regular**. Use the base form of a regular verb with *I, you, we,* and *they*.
Add *-s* or *-es* to the base form of the verb with *he, she,* or *it.*

I **grow.**	We **grow.**
You **grow.**	You **grow.**
He **grows.** She **grows.** It **grows.**	They **grow.**

I **watch.**	We **watch.**
You **watch.**	You **watch.**
He **watches.** She **watches.** It **watches.**	They **watch.**

Some verbs are **irregular**. Find the present forms of the verb *be* in the chart below.

I **am.**	We **are.**
You **are.**	You **are.**
He **is.** She **is.** It **is.**	They **are.**

Read the sentences. Circle the correct verb in parentheses ( ).

1. My little brother (am / is / are) two years old.

2. My parents (am / is / are) very proud of him.

3. Sometimes, I (am / is / are) a little jealous of the attention he gets.

4. Luckily, my parents are great. They (am / is / are) fair to both of us.

Complete each sentence with the correct present tense form of the verb in parentheses.

5. My uncle is fun; he _____ us twice a year. (visit)

6. He _____ wonderful stories. (tell)

7. They _____ always interesting. (be)

8. We _____ listening to him. (love)

9. He _____ us how to make up our own stories. (teach)

10. I _____ my uncle's only niece. (be)

Name _____   Date _____

SKILLS FOR WRITING

Use with textbook page 19.

Writing Correct Sentences
Use the words in the box to write a sentence. Add capital letters and punctuation.
Remember when two adjectives are used together, add a comma between them.

Example: | animals are hares / fast / furry | Hares are fast, furry animals.

1. | are runners hares fast |

_____

2. | slow tortoise steady the wins |

_____

3. | interesting cultures ancient are |

_____

4. | was ceremony the important |

_____

5. | arrives citizen the brave honest |

_____

6. | favorite is my fable funny |

_____

7. | amazing ancient an myth know I |

_____

8. | beautiful poems Homer wrote musical |

_____

9. | nap confident hare speedy took a the |

_____

10. | Greek was storyteller Aesop a great |

_____

PROOFREADING AND EDITING

Use with textbook page 20.

Read the sentences carefully. Find all the mistakes. Then rewrite the sentences correctly on the lines below.

      If you could travel back in time to Greece ancient, this are what you might see. The young people are learning to be citizens good. They is at school like young people today. They play with clay animals. Some children even have animals live.

      The life of young people then might be a lot like yours. They might be going to a school great, just as you is. At school, they learns to read and write. They plays with toys and have fun, too. Life different was then, but in some ways it are the same.

Name _____ Date _____

SPELLING

Use after the spelling lesson.

Short a, o, i

The vowel letters *a*, *i*, and *o* can stand for short vowel sounds. Read the words in the chart below.

Short *a*	Short *o*	Short *i*
m<u>a</u>n	j<u>o</u>b	b<u>i</u>g
<u>a</u>sk	n<u>o</u>t	r<u>i</u>ch
th<u>a</u>t	st<u>o</u>p	<u>i</u>n

Read the first word in each row of the chart below. Then read the other words in the row. Circle the word with the same short vowel sound as the first word.

1. that	ball	game	and
2. this	girl	with	life
3. not	top	boy	from
4. at	fast	father	army
5. it	write	six	kind

Read the words in the box below. Use the words to answer the questions. (Hint: You will not use all the words.)

wax	dish	mix	hot	boat	pass	fox
wish	dot	clay	fix	got	age	was

6. Which word has a short *a* sound and rhymes with *tax*? _____

7. What words have a short *i* sound and rhyme with *six*? _____

8. What words have a short *o* sound and rhyme with *not*? _____

9. What words have a short *i* sound and rhyme with *fish*? _____

10. Which word has a short *a* sound and rhymes with *glass*? _____

UNIT 1 Growing Up
PART 2

Contents

VOCABULARY

Use with textbook page 23.

Answer each question with a complete sentence. Use the **bold** word or phrase in your answer.

1. What **reptiles** might make good pets?

_____

2. What day is a **special** one for you?

_____

3. What can you do with a good **imagination**?

_____

4. What is a **normal** temperature on a hot summer day in Texas?

_____

5. Whom do you **get along with** and like to be with?

_____

6. What **birthday presents** would you like to get?

_____

Read the clues. Use the words in the box to complete the crossword puzzle. (Hint: You will not use all the words.)

imagination	grumbled	reptiles	normal
transparent	regular	special	tiring

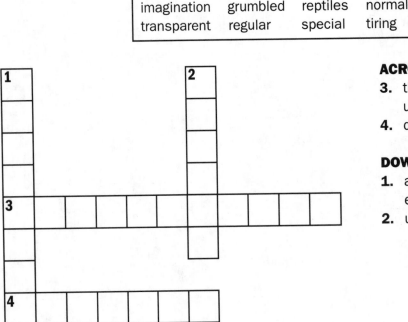

ACROSS
3. the ability to create or make up new ideas
4. different or unusual

DOWN
1. alligators and turtles, for example
2. usual

VOCABULARY BUILDING

Figurative Language

Sometimes writers use words to have more than a literal meaning.

Example: | When she spoke, her words were <u>icicles</u>.

Are the woman's words really icicles? How did she speak?

Read the words or the descriptions that Teddy uses in *Later, Gator*. Then write a brief answer to *a*. Write a complete sentence to answer *b*.

1. "Bobby's a regular mint chocolate bar."

   a. Use an adjective to describe the taste of a mint chocolate bar. _____

   b. Why does Teddy call Bobby a mint chocolate bar?

   _____

2. "And I am a raisin cookie."

   a. Which do most people like better, a raisin cookie or a mint chocolate bar?

   _____

   b. Why does Teddy call himself a raisin cookie, compared to Bobby?

   _____

3. Teddy calls Bobby a little angel.

   a. Use some adjectives to describe angels. _____

   b. What was something Bobby did that made him seem like an angel?

   _____

4. Teddy says that Bobby is a walking greeting card.

   a. Why do people like to get greeting cards? _____

   b. Why does Teddy call Bobby a greeting card?

   _____

5. Teddy said, "If there had been a light bulb over my head, it would have suddenly shone as bright as the sun."

   a. What does a light bulb over someone's head mean?_____

   b. What did Teddy's light bulb mean? _____

   _____

READING STRATEGY

Use with textbook page 23.

Predicting

When you read a story, it helps to think about what will happen next. Guessing what will happen is called **predicting**. Wondering what will happen makes a story more interesting. You can follow these steps to make predictions:

- Look for clues. The title or art might give you clues.
- Think about what you already know.
- Think about your own experiences.
- Make a prediction. What might happen next?
- Check your prediction later. Was your prediction correct?

Use these steps to predict what will happen in *Later, Gator* on pages 24–29 in your textbook.

Here are some questions to help you make predictions about the characters and what is happening in the story.

1. Read the title, the introduction, and the first paragraph on page 24 in your textbook.

   Is a character in the story telling it? How do you know? _____

   _____

2. Look at the picture on page 24 in your textbook. Which character, the younger boy or

   the older boy, has a problem or conflict? _____

   _____

3. Which character is happy? _____

   _____

4. On page 26, how would you describe the expression on the boy's face?

   _____

5. On page 28, what has caused the character's mood to change? _____

   _____

   _____

Remember to check your predictions after you read *Later, Gator.*

Use with textbook pages 32–34.

Summary: "Amazing Growth Facts"

This passage tells amazing facts about how different kinds of plants, animals, and people grow. Some things grow slowly, but other things grow very fast. Some facts compare human growth to plants' and animals' growth.

Visual Summary

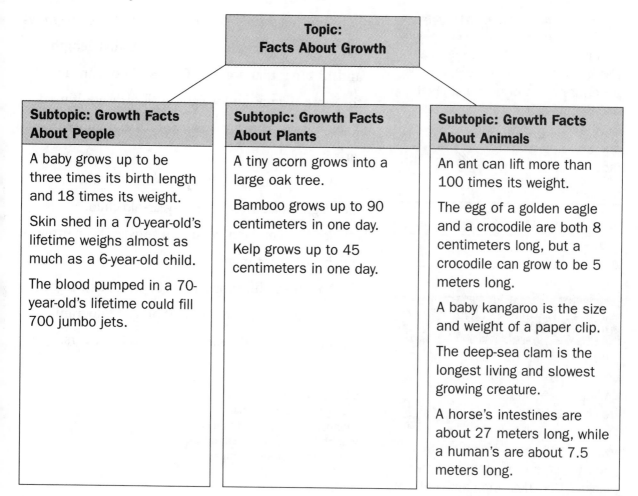

**Topic:
Facts About Growth**

Subtopic: Growth Facts About People

A baby grows up to be three times its birth length and 18 times its weight.

Skin shed in a 70-year-old's lifetime weighs almost as much as a 6-year-old child.

The blood pumped in a 70-year-old's lifetime could fill 700 jumbo jets.

Subtopic: Growth Facts About Plants

A tiny acorn grows into a large oak tree.

Bamboo grows up to 90 centimeters in one day.

Kelp grows up to 45 centimeters in one day.

Subtopic: Growth Facts About Animals

An ant can lift more than 100 times its weight.

The egg of a golden eagle and a crocodile are both 8 centimeters long, but a crocodile can grow to be 5 meters long.

A baby kangaroo is the size and weight of a paper clip.

The deep-sea clam is the longest living and slowest growing creature.

A horse's intestines are about 27 meters long, while a human's are about 7.5 meters long.

Amazing Growth Facts

It is one of the wonders of nature that all living things **increase** in size. Think about how a tiny acorn can grow into an enormous oak tree. Sometimes this growth is very fast, other times it is very slow.

The **average** newborn baby is 50 centimeters long and weighs 3.4 kilograms. When the baby grows up, he or she increases to three times that **length** and 18 times that **weight**. Girls and boys are about the same **height** and weight until early adulthood. Then boys usually grow taller and weigh more than girls.

Bamboo can grow 90 centimeters in one day— the height of an average three-year-old child.

Pacific giant kelp (a kind of seaweed) can grow as much as 45 centimeters in one day.

An ant can lift more than 100 times its weight. One hundred times the weight of a 64 kilogram person would be the same weight as three cars!

---

increase, become bigger
average, usual or normal
length, how long something is
weight, how heavy something is
height, how tall something is

Choose one and complete it.
1. Draw a picture of an acorn and an oak tree.
2. Research the growth of a plant or tree that interests you. Take notes.
3. Imagine you are a TV commentator reading the amazing growth facts on this page. Describe your tone of voice and any visuals you would show.

Text Structure: Informational Text

Sometimes, in an informational text, the writer asks questions. Underline the question on this page. Did you find yourself wondering about this?

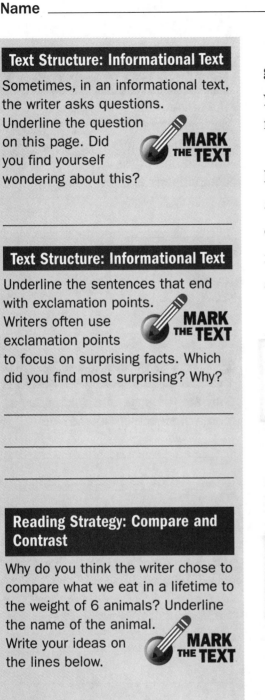 **MARK THE TEXT**

_____

Text Structure: Informational Text

Underline the sentences that end with exclamation points. Writers often use exclamation points to focus on surprising facts. Which did you find most surprising? Why?

MARK THE TEXT

_____

_____

_____

Reading Strategy: Compare and Contrast

Why do you think the writer chose to compare what we eat in a lifetime to the weight of 6 animals? Underline the name of the animal. Write your ideas on the lines below.

MARK THE TEXT

_____

_____

Comprehension Check

Why was this informational text called "Amazing Growth Facts"? What other title could you give it?

_____

_____

Clams are among the longest living and slowest growing of all **creatures**. A deep-sea clam takes 100 years to grow 8 millimeters. That's as big as your fingernail!

Do you ever wonder where the dust in your home comes from? Much of it **is made up of** the 50,000 or so microscopic **flakes** of skin that fall off of you every minute. All the skin **shed** by a person in a 70-year lifetime weighs almost as much as the average 6-year-old child (20 kilograms).

In the average human life of 70 years, a heart pumps enough blood around the body to fill the fuel tanks of 700 **jumbo jets**. The food that we eat in our lifetime is equal in weight to the weight of 6 elephants! A horse's **intestines** are about 27 meters long. A human's intestines are about 7.5 meters long. Luckily, the intestines are curled up inside the body. Otherwise, people and horses would look very strange!

_____

creatures, animals or insects
is made up of, consists of; contains
flakes, small, thin pieces
shed, lost by
jumbo jets, very big airplanes
intestines, tubes that take food from your stomach out of your body

Choose one and complete it.
1. Draw a picture to illustrate one of the amazing growth facts on this page.
2. Search the Internet. Find another amazing growth fact. Take notes about it.
3. Imagine you were a TV commentator reading the amazing growth facts on this page. Describe your tone of voice and any visuals you would show.

Name _____   Date _____

The egg of a golden eagle and the egg of a Nile crocodile are both 8 centimeters long. But the crocodile grows much bigger!

A 26-centimeter baby crocodile can grow into a 5-meter adult crocodile. If humans grew at the same **rate** as crocodiles, a 50-centimeter baby would grow into a 9.5-meter adult—more than 5 times as tall as the average person!

A baby kangaroo is the size and weight of a paper clip (1 gram). An adult kangaroo is 30,000 times heavier (30 kilograms). If a human grew at this rate, a 3.4-kilogram baby would weigh 102,000 kilograms as an adult—that's as much as a large whale! An average man weighs about 80 kilograms.

_____

rate, speed

Conversion Chart		
metric		**imperial**
1 millimeter	=	0.039 inches
1 centimeter	=	0.39 inches
1 meter	=	3.28 feet
1 gram	=	0.035 ounces
1 kilogram	=	2.2 pounds

Reading Strategy: Compare and Contrast

Underline what is being compared in each paragraph. Then choose one of the comparisons and rewrite it in your own words.

MARK THE TEXT

_____

_____

_____

_____

Comprehension Checks

Why are the eggs of a golden eagle and a crocodile compared?

_____

_____

_____

Why are crocodiles and humans compared?

_____

_____

_____

_____

Why are kangaroos and humans compared?

_____

_____

_____

Unit 1   Growing Up   Part 2   **21**

Retell It!

Choose four amazing growth facts. Write a riddle about each one. Here's an example:

In one day, I can grow to the height of an average three-year-old. What am I? *(bamboo)*

_____

_____

_____

_____

_____

_____

_____

Reader's Response

Which fact did you find most amazing? Tell why.

_____

_____

_____

_____

Think About the Skill

How did comparing and contrasting help you better understand the text?

_____

_____

_____

_____

_____

_____

_____

GRAMMAR

Use with textbook page 36.

The Conjunction *and*

The word ***and*** is a **conjunction**. A conjunction connects words, groups of words, and sentences. Read examples *A, B,* and *C.*

A. Use *and* to connect words in a sentence.

 Turtles and alligators are reptiles.

 A small and friendly turtle is a nice pet.

B. Use *and* to connect groups of words in a sentence.

 Teddy goes to the store and buys an alligator .

C. Use *and* to connect sentences. Place a comma before *and* when it connects two sentences.

 Bobby helps his father , and they work together at the fish shop .

Circle the conjunction in each sentence. Compare each sentence with examples **A, B,** and **C** above. Write the letter that shows how *and* is used. The first one has been done for you. Then complete the chart. Write the words, groups of words, or sentences that the conjunction connects.

1. Bobby likes turtles and fish. ____A____

	and	

2. Teddy reads the newspaper and sees an ad. _____

	and	

3. The alligators are small and hungry. _____

	and	

4. Teddy buys an alligator and brings it home. _____

	and	

5. Bobby is surprised, and Mother is angry. _____

	and	

Reminder: Which sentence needs a comma before *and*?

GRAMMAR

Use after the lesson about negative sentences.

Negative Sentences

Use **not** to make a sentence **negative**.

Teddy should buy Bobby a gift. ⟶ Teddy should *not* buy Bobby a gift.

Rewrite each sentence. Add *not* to make the sentence negative.

1. Teddy is jealous of Bobby.

_____

2. Bobby and Teddy are happy all the time.

_____

3. Pets should be dangerous.

_____

4. Bobby does like the alligator.

_____

Read the negative verbs and contractions.

is not ⟶ isn't   do not ⟶ don't   cannot ⟶ can't

are not ⟶ aren't   does not ⟶ doesn't   has not ⟶ hasn't

Rewrite each sentence. Change the underlined word or words to a contraction.

5. That <u>is not</u> fair! _____

6. I <u>do not</u> want to buy Bobby a present.

_____

7. He <u>has not</u> seen the gift yet.

_____

8. Alligators <u>are not</u> good pets.

_____

9. I <u>cannot</u> afford the official Willie Mays baseball glove.

_____

10. If he <u>does not</u> like it, can I return it?

_____

Name _____   Date _____

SKILLS FOR WRITING

Use with textbook page 37.

Writing Compound Sentences

Read the rules for writing **compound sentences** on page 37 in your textbook.

Read each sentence below. If the sentence is a compound sentence, circle *compound sentence*. If the sentence is not a compound sentence, circle *not a compound sentence*. Remember how a comma is used in a compound sentence.

1. Boys and girls are about the same weight when they are born.

compound sentence   not a compound sentence

2. The baby kangaroo heard a noise, looked up, and hopped away!

compound sentence   not a compound sentence

3. A crocodile appeared, and all the birds flew away.

compound sentence   not a compound sentence

4. Crocodiles swim in swamps, rivers, and streams.

compound sentence   not a compound sentence

5. Clams have hard shells, and they grow very slowly.

compound sentence   not a compound sentence

6. Bamboo grows on land, and kelp grows underwater.

compound sentence   not a compound sentence

Write four compound sentences using the conjunction *and*. Be sure to punctuate correctly.

7. _____

_____

8. _____

_____

9. _____

_____

10. _____

_____

PROOFREADING AND EDITING

Use with textbook page 38.

Read each sentence carefully. Decide if the punctuation is correct. Find the mistakes. Then rewrite the paragraph correctly on the lines below.

Maggie, and I saw something fantastic today! We went to the zoo. and we watched baby alligators hatch. They broke their eggs and they crawled out. They are tiny green, and beautiful. They bark and squeak. The babies are'nt big. They are small, fragile, and adorable. They stay in the nest and they wait for their mother. The mother alligator is big, strong and dangerous. She does'nt want anyone near her babies. She growled at us and we left her alone. A photographer and, his assistant were at the zoo, too. They took pictures of the alligators crocodiles and turtles. Their best photo was one of the mother alligator, and her babies. The baby alligators were crawling around the nest. and the mother was watching them.

The babies will grow into adults and be like their mother. The mother will lay new eggs and she will have another new family of baby alligators.

_____

_____

_____

_____

_____

_____

_____

_____

_____

_____

SPELLING

Use after the spelling lesson.

Spelling Short *u* and *e*

Some words with short *u* and short *e* follow these patterns.

Pattern	Short *u*	Short *e*
C-V-C (Consonant-Vowel-Consonant)	fun	pet
C-V-C-C (Consonant-Vowel-Consonant-Consonant)	jump	send

Read the following sentences from the selection. Look for the bold word with a missing letter. Decide whether to use a short *e* or *u* to make a word that fits the sentence. Write the missing letter. Then in the space provided, write the pattern. The first one has been done for you.

C-V-C-C   **1.** Bobby was too **d _u_ mb** to understand the insult.

_____   **2.** "They're neat-o and **j __ st** what I wanted."

_____   **3.** Bobby had to **p __ t** on his new socks right away and wriggle his toes at me.

_____   **4.** "Why can't you **g __ t** along with your little brother?"

_____   **5.** "You can buy him a **p __ t**."

_____   **6.** Instead, I just **h __ ng** around the apartment and moped.

_____   **7.** After Father and Bobby **l __ ft** for work, Mother stood over me.

_____   **8.** "I **c __ t** out the ad from the newspaper so you would know where to go."

_____   **9.** If there had been a light **b __ lb** over my head, it would have suddenly shone

as bright as the sun.

_____   **10.** He would probably **r __ n** shrieking from the room.

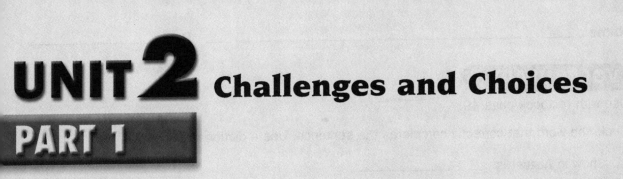

UNIT 2 Challenges and Choices

PART 1

Contents

VOCABULARY

Use with textbook page 49.

Circle the word that correctly completes the sentence. Use a dictionary if needed.

1. Snow in August is _____.

    uncommon   ordinary   incapable

2. A dog is _____ of talking.

    extraordinary   incapable   disability

3. Jeremy did an _____ thing by running a marathon only six months after breaking his leg.

    extraordinary   underachiever   incapable

4. Victor is smart, but he gets average grades because he is a(n) _____.

    unusual   uncommon   underachiever

5. A determined person can overcome a(n) _____.

    extraordinary   ordinary   disability

Read the clues and complete the crossword puzzle. (Hint: You will not use all the words.)

unusual	separate	incapable	extraordinary
underachiever	compete	uncommon	disability

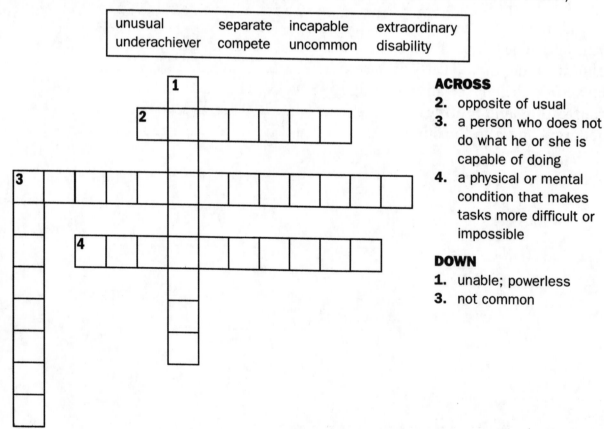

ACROSS

2. opposite of usual

3. a person who does not do what he or she is capable of doing

4. a physical or mental condition that makes tasks more difficult or impossible

DOWN

1. unable; powerless

3. not common

VOCABULARY BUILDING

Understanding Prefixes

A **prefix** is a letter or letters added to the beginning of a word that changes the word's meaning. A prefix added to a word forms a new word.

Prefix	Meaning
un-	not
extra-	more than usual; beyond
dis-	opposite of
in-	not
under-	below; beneath

Use the meaning of the prefixes to define each new word.

Prefix	+	Word	=	New Word	Meaning

1. dis- + honest = _____ _____

2. un- + ending = _____ _____

3. under- + valued = _____ _____

4. in- + complete = _____ _____

5. extra- + curricular = _____ _____

Read the questions and answers in this interview with an astronaut. Underline each word that has a prefix. Then complete the chart. Write the word, the prefix, and the meaning of the word. Check the meaning of the prefix in the chart above. Then use a dictionary to check your answers.

Interviewer: What is it like to be an astronaut?

Astronaut: It's extraordinary. Traveling in space gives you an unreal feeling.

Interviewer: Can you tell us about that feeling?

Astronaut: In space, your earthly worries go away.

Interviewer: Is there anything you dislike about your job?

Astronaut: Much hard work underlies my job. It would be inaccurate to say it doesn't. But it is the most thrilling job in the world!

Word	Prefix	Meaning
6.		
7.		
8.		
9.		
10.		

READING STRATEGY

Use with textbook page 49.

Skimming a Text to Determine Major Ideas

Skimming a text gives you an idea of what the text will be about. A quick skim helps you get ready to read. To skim a text:

- Read it quickly to get the main ideas only.
- Skip words you don't know.

After you skim, you will have some idea of what the text will be about. Then you can begin a careful reading.

Skim "Extraordinary People." Then match each person with the correct description. Write the letter on the line.

_____ **1.** Rosa Parks

_____ **2.** Albert Einstein

_____ **3.** Stephen Hawking

_____ **4.** Robert Peary

_____ **5.** Helen Keller

_____ **6.** Wolfgang Amadeus Mozart

_____ **7.** Ellen Ochoa

_____ **8.** Adriana Fernandez

_____ **9.** Erik Weihenmayer

a. first sight- and hearing-impaired person to graduate from college

b. physicist and author of *A Brief History of Time*

c. a sight-impaired mountain climber who made it to the top of Mount Everest

d. probably one of the first people to reach the North Pole

e. person who helped the cause of civil rights by refusing to move from a seat on a segregated bus

f. astronaut who has flown on three space missions

g. physicist who was an underachiever at school

h. one of history's greatest composers

i. famous runner who won the 1999 New York City Marathon

10. Think about the main idea of "Extraordinary People." Why is it included in this unit about challenges and choices?

_____

_____

_____

_____

_____

_____

Use with textbook pages 58–60.

Summary: "He Was the Same Age as My Sister"

This selection describes an autumn afternoon in Holland, near the end of World War II. The author tells about a surprising experience she had with a young German soldier.

Visual Summary

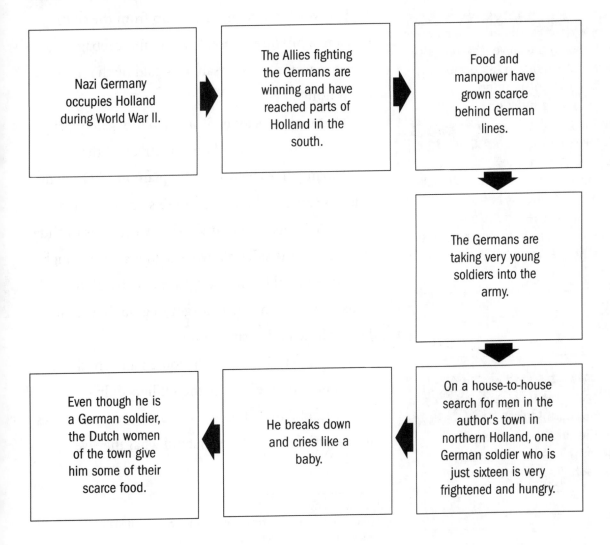

Use What You Know

List three things you know about World War II.

1. _____

2. _____

3. _____

Text Structure: Personal Narrative

In a personal narrative, the narrator tells about events in his or her own life. The narrator is often an older person looking back on something that happened years before. Underline the words in the first paragraph that tell how old the narrator is now and how old she was when the events happened. What happens now that makes her remember those events?

_____

_____

_____

Reading Strategy: Skimming a Text

Skim the first three paragraphs. Look for the main ideas of each paragraph. Then list the main ideas here.

_____

_____

_____

_____

_____

_____

He Was the Same Age as My Sister
by Mieke C. Malandra

I'm nearly sixty-seven years old, but every October when the weather **turns**, I am eleven again.

In the last year of the war, fall in Holland was cold and wet. No lighted stoves, no coal. No lamps to make the room seem warm, no electricity. No supper worth the name. The soup from the central kitchen, a mixture of potato peels and cabbage leaves in water without salt, was cold by the time we got it home.

That day in October, just when it began to get dark, army trucks closed off our street, as they had done many times before, and a **platoon** of German soldiers started a house-to-house search for men.

"**Raus**! Raus!" The **loudspeaker** drove us outside to stand on the sidewalk while soldiers ran through our houses, poking in **attics** and closets. "Raus! Raus!" My little brothers forgot to grab their coats. Jacob's little body warmed me.

Our street filled up with women and children. We could talk freely, since the soldiers didn't understand Dutch, but we kept our voices low. Jokes flew around. I didn't understand what they were

---

turns, changes
platoon, part of an army commanded by a lieutenant
raus, German for "get out"
loudspeaker, piece of equipment that makes a person's voice louder
attics, rooms at the top of a house under the roof

talking about, but I liked the laughter. Then news was exchanged. They're in Maastricht! Why won't they come north?

It got colder. The soldiers had nearly come to the end of the street, and no men had been found. We became quiet. And then we heard someone crying. All the mothers turned. It was the sound of a crying child. On the stoop of Mr. van Campen's house sat a soldier, his rifle propped up next to him, his face hidden in his coat. He tried to swallow his sobs, but then he gave up.

_____

stoop, stairway or porch at the entrance of a house
sobs, the sound someone makes when crying

Choose one and complete it.
1. Draw a map to help you understand where Holland, Maastricht (Belgium), and Germany are. Research the map in an atlas or on the Internet.
2. Do research to find out more about Holland during World War II. Take notes on the information you find.
3. Imagine that you and some classmates are acting out the incident the author tells about. What sound effects might you use in the background? List your ideas.

Comprehension Check
The women and children of the town speak Dutch, the language of Holland. Underline the news that they exchange. In the news, who are "they," and what are "they" doing?

_____
_____
_____
_____

Literary Element: Mood
The mood of a work is its atmosphere or feeling. Circle two words on this page that help create the mood. What sort of mood is it?

_____

Text Structure: Personal Narrative
In a personal narrative, the narrator is a character in the work. This means the narrator uses first-person pronouns like *I* and *me* to talk about himself or herself. To talk about himself or herself along with other characters, the narrator uses plural first-person pronouns like *we* and *us*. Underline three first-person pronouns the narrator uses on these pages. When the narrator uses *we* or *us*, whom does she mean?

_____
_____

Comprehension Check

Circle the question that the Dutch woman asks the young soldier. Then underline what she tells the others. 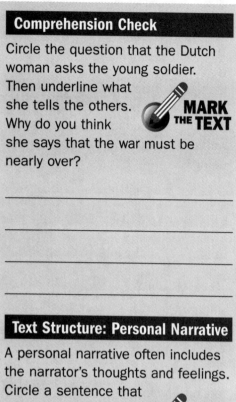 Why do you think she says that the war must be nearly over?

_____

_____

_____

_____

Text Structure: Personal Narrative

A personal narrative often includes the narrator's thoughts and feelings. Circle a sentence that tells what the narrator thinks or feels when an officer comes near. What does the last sentence show that the narrator thinks or feels about the young German soldier?

_____

_____

_____

Reading Strategy: Skimming a Text

Skim the page to find three things the Dutch women give the young German soldier. List them here.

1. _____

2. _____

3. _____

A mother walked over and talked to him softly in German. "What's wrong?" she asked. She bent over him as he spoke, and when he was finished, she stood straight up and **announced** to us, "This war must nearly be over. He's sixteen years old and hasn't had anything to eat today." Two or three mothers slipped away from the group and went into their houses. A German officer came walking down the street half a **block** away. I was scared—and very cold. The mothers managed to get back in time. A cold cooked potato, a piece of bread, and a wrinkled apple were passed through the group to the boy.

The officer came closer. The boy turned into a soldier again. "**Danke**," he said, and then climbed to his feet and grabbed his rifle.

The truck engines started up. We could go inside. For the rest of the war, for the rest of my life, I have remembered that soldier who cried. He was the same age as my sister.

_____

announced, told
block, the distance between two streets
danke, German for "thank you"

Name _____ Date _____

Retell It!

Imagine that the German soldier is now a man in his seventies. Retell the events from his point of view.

_____

_____

_____

_____

_____

_____

_____

_____

_____

Reader's Response

Would you have helped the young German soldier if you were one of the Dutch women? Tell what you would have done and why.

_____

_____

_____

_____

_____

Think About the Skill

How did skimming this personal narrative help you understand it?

_____

_____

_____

_____

_____

GRAMMAR

Use with textbook page 62.

The Simple Past

To form the **simple past** of most regular verbs, add *-ed* to the base form. Complete the charts. Follow the examples. Review the rules and charts for forming the simple past of verbs in your textbook on page 62.

talk	+ -ed	talked
wonder	+ -ed	**1.**

look	+ -ed	looked
discover	+ -ed	**2.**

For regular verbs that end with a silent *-e*, add *-d* to form the simple past.

smile	+ -d	smiled
explore	+ -d	**3.**

race	+ -d	raced
achieve	+ -d	**4.**

Read this paragraph. Circle the regular verbs that are in the simple past. Underline the irregular past-tense verbs.

> The runners crouched at the starting line. At the loud signal, the race started. Adriana Fernandez ran smoothly and gracefully. She stayed in the middle for most of the race. Then she made her move. She passed one runner and then another. She flew past the woman in the lead. Adriana won the race!

In the chart, list the verbs you circled and underlined above. In the right column, write the type of verb, regular or irregular.

Verb	Type
5.	**6.**
7.	**8.**
9.	**10.**
11.	**12.**

Verb	Type
13.	**14.**
15.	**16.**
17.	**18.**
19.	**20.**

GRAMMAR

Use after the lesson on parts of speech.

Identifying Parts of Speech

Read the following passage from the selection *He Was the Same Age as My Sister*. Then, for each part of speech defined below it, list two examples from the passage. For the interjection, just list one example.

> "Raus! Raus!" The loudspeaker drove us outside to stand on the sidewalk while soldiers ran through our houses, poking in attics and closets. "Raus! Raus!" My little brothers forgot to grab their coats. Jacob's little body warmed me.
>
> Our street filled up with women and children. We could talk freely, since the soldiers didn't understand Dutch, but we kept our voices low. Jokes flew around. I didn't understand what they were talking about, but I liked the laughter. Then news was exchanged. They're in Maastricht! Why won't they come north?
>
> It got colder. The soldiers had nearly come to the end of the street, and no men had been found. We became quiet.

1. A **noun** (*n.*) names a person, place, or thing.

   _____   _____

2. A **verb** (*v.*) shows an action.

   _____   _____

3. A **pronoun** (*pron.*) replaces a noun.

   _____   _____

4. An **adjective** (*adj.*) describes a noun or pronoun.

   _____   _____

5. An **adverb** (*adv.*) tells how an action is done.

   _____   _____

6. A **conjunction** (*conj.*) joins two or more parts of a sentence.

   _____   _____

7. A **preposition** (*prep.*) shows a relationship, often a location or position.

   _____   _____

8. An **interjection** (*interj.*) expresses strong emotion. _____

9. Underline two more nouns, different from the ones you listed above.

10. Underline two more pronouns, different from the ones you listed above.

SKILLS FOR WRITING

Use with textbook page 63.

Narrative Writing

In a **narrative**, events are usually told in chronological order. Complete the paragraph using the words and phrases from the box. These words show sequence or time order. You can use the same word or phrase more than once. You will not use all of the words.

First	Second	Third	Next
At first	After that	Then	Finally

My Extraordinary Neighbor

Jared is my neighbor. He repairs cars. He can repair any problem with

a car. Last year, my mother bought a used car. _____*At first*_____, it

drove very well. _____1_____, it started making a funny noise.

_____2_____, the door stopped opening. _____3_____,

the engine died._____4_____, my mother gave up and asked Jared

for help. He fixed the car in just two days. _____5_____, the car

was perfect.

Write four sentences describing something you did last week using the order in which you did it.

6. First, I _____

   _____

7. Then I _____

   _____

8. Next, I _____

   _____

9. After that, I _____

   _____

10. Finally, I _____

    _____

PROOFREADING AND EDITING

Read the following narrative carefully. Find all the mistakes. Rewrite the narrative composition correctly on the lines below.

My amazing Grandmother

My grandmother is the most extra ordinary person I know. She born in mexico. Then, she moved to california when she was 11. She did not speak no English.

Next, she meeted a man named Dr. Rodriguez when she was fourteen. dr. Rodriguez was the school Doctor. He sees that my grandmother was very inteligent. He suggest that she study biology. then she became his assistant at school.

my Grandmother decide to became a doctor years later. Then, she went to medical school. She studied every night. Finally, she graduate from medical school. She became a wonderful childrens doctor.

_____

_____

_____

_____

_____

_____

_____

_____

_____

_____

_____

_____

_____

SPELLING

Use after the spelling lesson.

Long *a* and *i* Sounds

The long *a* sound can be spelled in different ways. Look at these examples.

Pattern	Examples
a-e	same, rate
ay	may, today

The long *i* sound can also be spelled with different patterns. Here is one of the most common spelling patterns for long *i*.

Pattern	Examples
i-e	time, life

Read the first word in each row. Then read the other words in the row. Circle the word with the same long vowel sound as the first word.

1. same	half	back	away
2. time	why	since	him
3. gave	face	grab	coat
4. child	cry	piece	slipped
5. cave	grabbed	age	talk
6. straight	eat	sat	name

Rearrange the letters to form a word with the long *a* or long *i* sound. Use the clues in parentheses ( ). Then use each word in a sentence.

7. Y S A (clue: long *a* spelled *ay*) _____

_____

8. E T W I R (clue: long *i* spelled *i–e*) _____

_____

9. A T E L (clue: long *a* spelled *a–e*)_____

_____

10. E I V A L (clue: long *i* spelled *i–e*)_____

_____

UNIT 2 Challenges and Choices

PART 2

Contents

VOCABULARY

Use with textbook page 67.

Read the sentences about some of the characters you will read about in the excerpt from *A Boat to Nowhere*. Think about the meaning of the **boldfaced** words. Then use these words as clues to answer the questions.

Their grandfather decides to take Loc and Mai and **run away** from the city and the war.

Hong tells the starved Kien that his **belly** will explode if he eats more.

Mai has only a little **memory** of her father and mother.

The war-torn country had made **beggars** of many, but Kien would work for his food.

Kien sings a song about cannons and **rifles** coming closer.

_____ **1.** Who can barely remember others in the past?

_____ **2.** Who does not want to get his food for free?

_____ **3.** Who tells Kien that he has already eaten too much?

_____ **4.** Who hints to the villagers that firearms are approaching?

_____ **5.** Who takes others and leaves a place of trouble?

Read the clues and complete the crossword puzzle. (Hint: You will not use all of the words.)

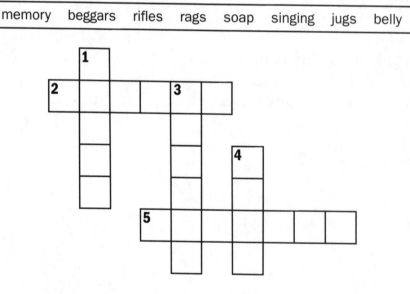

| memory | beggars | rifles | rags | soap | singing | jugs | belly |

ACROSS
2. something remembered
5. people who ask for food or money

DOWN
1. stomach
3. firearms
4. clothing in poor condition

VOCABULARY BUILDING

Understanding Suffixes

A **suffix** is a letter or group of letters added to the end of some words. A suffix changes the meaning of the word. Knowing the meaning of suffixes helps you understand the meaning of words.

Suffix	Meaning	Example
-er, -or, -ar	someone who does something	conqueror (someone who conquers)
-less	without	thoughtless (without thought)
-ly	a way of doing something	impudently (in an impudent, rude, or disrespectful way)

Circle the suffix in each word. Then write the meaning of the word.

1. homeless _____

2. teacher _____

3. suddenly _____

4. unfriendly _____

5. heartless _____

Sometimes the spelling changes when you add a suffix. Make new words by making the changes shown. Then write the meaning of the new word. Use a dictionary if needed.

6. In a one-syllable word with a short e sound, double the ending consonant.

    beg + g + ar = _____, meaning: _____

7. In a word ending in a silent e, drop the silent e before adding -er, -ar, or -or.

    village + er = _____, meaning: _____

8. In some words ending in le, drop the le before adding -ly.

    terrible + ly = _____, meaning: _____

9. In a word ending in y, if the letter before the y is a consonant, change the y to i before adding ly.

    busy + i + ly = _____, meaning: _____

10. In a word ending in silent e, if the letter before it is c, change the ce to t before adding ly.

    silence + t + ly = _____, meaning: _____

READING STRATEGY

Use with textbook page 67.

Visualizing

When you **visualize**, you picture something in your mind. Writers use descriptive words to help readers visualize the characters, setting, and events of a story.

Read the first page of the excerpt from *A Boat to Nowhere* on page 69 of your textbook. Visualize how the characters look, act, and say their words.

• watched amazed
• wolfed down
• four big bowls of rice
• grumbled
• "Now, move!"
• snort of laughter
• snapped
• slurped

• scooping it up
• shrugged
• couldn't help staring
• blushed
• lice and fleas
• paid no attention
• burn those rags

Choose words or groups of words from the chart that help you visualize how the characters look, act, speak, and react.

1. Write four words or groups of words that help you visualize how hungry Kien is.

_____

_____

2. Write two words or groups of words that help you visualize how dirty Kien is.

_____

_____

3. Write three words or groups of words that help you visualize Mai's reactions to Kien.

_____

_____

4. Write three words or groups of words that help visualize how Hong speaks to Kien.

_____

_____

5. Write three words or groups of words that help you visualize Kien's reactions to the others.

_____

_____

Use with textbook pages 76–78.

Summary: "Sudan's 'Lost Boys' Start New Lives"

This magazine article tells about a group of children from Sudan called the "Lost Boys." In 1987 and 1988, about 20,000 boys and 2,000 girls left Sudan because of a war. The children walked through the East African desert to find a safe place to live. Now the "Lost Boys" are young men, and some are starting new lives in the United States.

Visual Summary

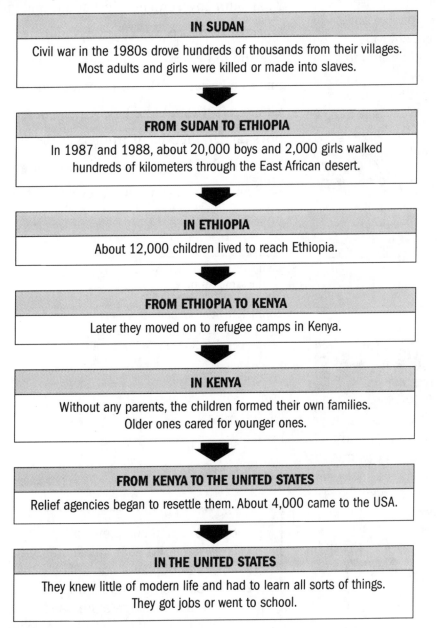

IN SUDAN

Civil war in the 1980s drove hundreds of thousands from their villages. Most adults and girls were killed or made into slaves.

FROM SUDAN TO ETHIOPIA

In 1987 and 1988, about 20,000 boys and 2,000 girls walked hundreds of kilometers through the East African desert.

IN ETHIOPIA

About 12,000 children lived to reach Ethiopia.

FROM ETHIOPIA TO KENYA

Later they moved on to refugee camps in Kenya.

IN KENYA

Without any parents, the children formed their own families. Older ones cared for younger ones.

FROM KENYA TO THE UNITED STATES

Relief agencies began to resettle them. About 4,000 came to the USA.

IN THE UNITED STATES

They knew little of modern life and had to learn all sorts of things. They got jobs or went to school.

Use What You Know

List three things you know about immigrants who come to America.

1. _____

2. _____

3. _____

Text Structure: Magazine Article

A magazine article is a short piece of writing about real people and events. Like newspaper stories, magazine articles often tell *who, what, when, where, why,* and *how*. Circle the details that tell you who the article is about, what they did, why they did it, when they did it, where they did it, and how they did it. Sum up the information. **MARK THE TEXT**

_____

_____

_____

Reading Strategy: Visualizing and Drawing Conclusions

Visualizing means picturing something you read or hear about. Writers use descriptive words to help you visualize what they write. Underline three details that help you visualize the children's walk through the East African desert. What words would you use to describe that walk? List two.  **MARK THE TEXT**

1. _____

2. _____

Sudan's "Lost Boys" Start New Lives

Since the mid-1980s, the people of Sudan have experienced terrible civil war caused by religious, ethnic, and regional conflict. In 1987 and 1988, about 20,000 boys and 2,000 girls left their villages in southern Sudan. They left because their villages were destroyed by troops from the northern Khartoum government. Most adults and girls were killed or sold as slaves. The boys, mostly between five and ten years old, had nowhere to go and no one to take care of them. They walked hundreds of kilometers through the East African desert. Some boys carried their baby brothers as they walked. Many died of hunger, thirst, disease, or attack by wild animals. To stay alive, they often ate leaves and mud.

---

civil war, war between two or more groups of people who live in the same country
ethnic, racial or cultural
conflict, fight or argument
troops, soldiers; members of the army
slaves, people who are sold for money

Choose one and complete it.
1. Research the East African desert. Draw pictures of plants and animals there.
2. Do research on the Internet to find out more about temperatures and conditions in the East African desert. Take notes.

About 12,000 children reached Ethiopia. In
Ethiopia, and later in Kenya, they lived in refugee
camps for over ten years. They didn't have any
parents, so the children formed their own "family"
groups. The older children took care of the younger
ones. Relief workers in the camps named the
children the "Lost Boys." This name comes from the
book *Peter Pan*. In *Peter Pan*, a group of boys stays
together without adults.

Now most of these "lost boys" are young
men between seventeen and twenty-five years old.
About 4,000 of them have moved to the United
States. First, the young men fly from Kenya to the
United States. Relief organizations are helping the
men start a new life in freedom and safety.

One organization, World Vision, is helping
about fifty young Sudanese men settle in the Seattle
area of Washington. World Vision first places each
young man with an American family for two to four
weeks. Then the young men move into apartments.
They study English and learn about American
culture. They must learn all aspects of American life
(from using a can opener to finding a job) very
quickly. That way, they can learn to live
independently. This is a very difficult task,
especially when they have never seen mattresses,
lightbulbs, ice, or a television.

---

refugee camps, temporary living areas for people who have to
   leave their homes because of war
relief workers, people who help victims of a disaster
organizations, groups such as clubs or businesses
settle, begin to live in a new place
aspects, parts of a situation, idea, problem, etc.
independently, alone, without help

Comprehension Check

Circle the origin of the name "Lost Boys." How did the name apply to these children?

Reading Strategy: Visualizing and Recognizing Details

Underline two sentences that help you visualize where the "Lost Boys" went after leaving Africa. About how old were they by then?

Comprehension Check

Circle five things the "Lost Boys" learned about after coming to the United States. Based on what they didn't know, what can you conclude about their lives in the refugee camps?

Comprehension Check

Underline the word that best describes the reaction the "Lost Boys" had when they first saw keys, stoves, stairs, and telephones. What three other things does the paragraph say caused the same reaction? **MARK THE TEXT**

1. _____

2. _____

3. _____

Reading Strategy: Visualizing and Drawing Conclusions

Circle three details that help you visualize what the "Lost Boys" did to the refrigerator. How do you think they felt when they saw all the food inside? Why? **MARK THE TEXT**

_____

_____

_____

Text Structure: Magazine Article

Magazine articles often have pictures to show examples of statements made. What pictures might you use to give examples of the first sentence of the last paragraph?

_____

_____

_____

_____

Since they arrived, the young men have been amazed by new discoveries: keys, stoves, stairs, and telephones. Then there is macaroni, canned juice, and the "huge white box" in the kitchen. They tried lifting the strange machine from the bottom. They tried pulling it apart. Then they discovered the handle and opened the refrigerator. It was full of cold, unfamiliar foods.

Some of the young men will use their time in the United States to get a good education and earn money. Then they hope to return to Sudan and rebuild their villages.

Choose one and complete it.
1. Draw a map to help you understand how far the children walked. Research the map in an atlas or on the Internet.
2. Do research to find out more about the East African desert the children crossed. Take notes on the information you find.
3. Imagine that you are creating a TV documentary about the "Lost Boys." Which scenes would you show? List your ideas.

Name _____ Date _____

Imagine one of the "Lost Boys" is describing his experiences to classmates in college. List details of his story.

_____

_____

_____

_____

_____

_____

Reader's Response

If one of the "Lost Boys" had stayed with your family right after coming to the United States, what interesting thing would you have shown him? Why?

_____

_____

_____

_____

_____

_____

Think About the Skill

How did visualizing help you better understand this magazine article?

_____

_____

_____

_____

_____

_____

GRAMMAR

Use with textbook page 80.

The Conjunction *but*

Read the two examples of ways to use the conjunction *but*.

To connect contrasting adjectives: *The rice was plain **but** tasty.*

To combine contrasting sentences: *Kien was rude, **but** Mai was friendly.*

Combine the two sentences into one simple sentence. Use *but* to connect contrasting adjectives.

1. The village was small. The village was beautiful.

   _____

2. Kien was young. Kien was hardened by the war.

   _____

3. Mai was curious. She was shy at first.

   _____

4. Mai and Loc were scared. They were brave.

   _____

5. Hong was helpful. She was busy.

   _____

Use a comma and the conjunction *but* to form compound sentences.

6. Her father was gone. Mai remembered him.

   _____

7. Mai lived in the small village. She once lived in a city.

   _____

8. Hong was easily upset. She was kind.

   _____

9. Hong had clean clothes for Kien. He had to bathe first.

   _____

10. The people of the village had felt safe. Kien brought fearful news.

   _____

GRAMMAR

Use after the lesson on questions in the past and present.

Questions in Present and Past

- Some questions in the present are formed with this pattern:

  Do, Does, or *Can* + a subject + the base form of a verb

  You want a bowl of rice. ➤ *Do* you want a bowl of rice?

  Mai lives here. ➤ *Does* Mai live here?

  Loc can walk now. ➤ *Can* Loc walk now?

- Some questions in the past are formed with this pattern:

  Did + a subject + the base form of a verb or an adjective

  Kien ate too much. ➤ *Did* Kien eat too much?

Rewrite each sentence as a question. Begin with the word given.

1. Kien wants another bowl of rice.

Does _____

2. Mai and Hong think that Kien is rude.

Do _____

3. You can guess what will happen next.

Can _____

4. Kien ate everything in sight.

Did _____

5. Mai helps Hong in the kitchen area.

Does _____

6. Readers understood the characters.

Did _____

7. Mai and Kien become friends.

Do _____

8. Mai and Loc escaped several years ago.

Did _____

9. Mai can remember her mother and father.

Can _____

10. Their grandfather lives with them.

Does _____

SKILLS FOR WRITING

Use with textbook page 81.

Using a Variety of Sentences

Writers use time order words to make the sequence easy to follow. For example, they use *recently, first, then,* and *finally.* They also use the conjunctions *but* and *and* to combine simple sentences into compound sentences.

In the paragraph, underline the words that show the sequence more clearly. Circle the conjunctions that form compound sentences. (Hint: there are five of each.)

Simon lived in southern Sudan, but he had to leave his village. First, he
1 **2**

just tried to stay alive. Finally he made it to Ethiopia. Later he went to a
3 **4**

refugee camp in Kenya, and there he found a home for several years. He
5

met other refugees, but there were few families. Most were other boys like
6

him. Soon they formed their own families, and they became known as the
7 **8**

"Lost Boys." Now they are older, but they will never forget their amazing
9 **10**

experience of survival.

Use the word or words in parentheses ( ). Combine sentences using conjunctions. Use the time words to show the sequence clearly. (Hint: Use commas correctly.)

11. The young men wanted to come to the U.S. Some wanted to return to Sudan to

help. (Earlier/Later) _____

12. Their lives were difficult in Sudan. They faced challenges in the United States, too.

(but) _____

13. The Sudanese had never needed keys. They had never used a telephone.

(and) _____

14. They tried to pull a refrigerator apart. They discovered the handle.

(First/Then)_____

15. Some returned to Sudan. Others stayed in the United States.

(Later/but) _____

PROOFREADING AND EDITING

Use with textbook page 82.

Read about a student's personal experience. Watch for errors in forming questions, using the conjunction *but*, using time order words, adding suffixes to words, verb form, punctuation, spelling, and capitalization. Find all the mistakes. Then rewrite the composition correctly on the lines below.

My Rewarding Experiance

Does you know about World Vision. Today, I volunteered to help at their headquarters here in seattle. It is a small but, important agency. World Vision started here. But it helps people around the World.

Last, when I arrived there, the janiter showed me around. Then I began working. Later, I meet some men who where helped by World Vision. They spoke sad about their memories. In Africa, their village were destroyed, leaving them home less. Their mothers and sisters were tragical taken away but somehow the young men survived. Finaly World Vision helped them come to America.

I heard other storys that make me want to volenteer again soon. They can use more helpers. You can spare an afternoon?

_____

_____

_____

_____

_____

_____

_____

_____

_____

_____

_____

_____

Name _____ Date _____

SPELLING

Use after the spelling lesson.

Long o, Long e, and Long u

Look at the chart below to see ways to spell long o, long e, and long u. One spelling pattern is the 2-vowel rule where the first vowel letter stands for the long vowel sound. In words with the VCe pattern, the e is silent and the first vowel letter stands for the long vowel sound.

Pattern	Long o	Long e	Long u
2-vowel rule	boat	lean	dues
VCe	poke	compete	rude

Write the words in the correct column of the chart below. Put a check mark (✔) in the box for the pattern of each word.

1. boast	**5.** soap	**9.** clues	**13.** complete
2. fleas	**6.** home	**10.** huge	**14.** leaves
3. mean	**7.** clean	**11.** seen	**15.** use
4. stoves	**8.** mule	**12.** tube	**16.** wrote

Long o	(2-vowel) rule	(VCe)	Long e	(2-vowel) rule	(VCe)	long u	(2-vowel) rule	(VCe)

Write a word with each pattern. Then use the word in a sentence.

17. Long o: _____oa_____(2-vowel rule)

_____

18. Long u: _____u_____e (VCe)

_____

19. Long e: _____ea_____ (2-vowel rule)

_____

20. Long o: _____o_____e (VCe)

_____

UNIT 3 Mysterious Ways

PART 1

Contents

NoneNameNoneNoneNoneNoneNone Date NoneNoneNoneNone

VOCABULARY

Use with textbook page 93.

Use the words in the box to complete the story.

sacred	archaeologist	creature	fantasy	clues

Dr. Haller was a famous _____. She studied ancient cultures.
                                    1

She found ancient objects that gave her _____ to the way people lived
                                                            2

long ago. In Egypt, she found a stone statue. It was a carving of a strange

_____ with a cat's head and a person's body. Dr. Haller knew that cats
       3

were _____ in Egypt. The Egyptians believed cats were holy.
               4

After her discovery, Dr. Haller saw what looked like a cat with human arms and legs.

Dr. Haller closed her eyes and shook her head in disbelief. Then she looked again. It was

gone. Was the cat-person real? No, it must have been just a _____.
                                                                      5

Read the definitions. Use words from the box to complete the crossword puzzle. Hint: You
will not use all the words.

disappeared	places	sacred	encyclopedias	fingerprint
archaeologist	building	fantasy	creature	ancient

ACROSS
3. something unreal
5. a person who studies
   ancient cultures

DOWN
1. vanished; went away
2. holy; blessed
4. a living being, human
   or animal

58None Unit 3 Mysterious Ways Part 1

VOCABULARY BUILDING

Understanding Synonyms

Synonyms are words that have the same or nearly the same meaning. Look at the examples listed in the chart below.

Synonyms	
large	big
fast	quickly
gift	present
speak	talk

Read the first word in each row. Then circle its synonym.

1. tiny   small   huge   flat

2. mystery   trouble   puzzle   party

3. ancient   new   young   old

4. strange   peculiar   plain   common

Synonyms provide you with choices when you write or speak. Read the paragraph below. Then write a synonym for each underlined word in the space provided below. You can use synonyms from the box or choose your own. You may wish to use a thesaurus or synonym finder.

mystery	treasures	ancient	pharaoh's
beautiful	discovered	tomb	

Tutankhamen was a ruler in <u>old</u> Egypt. He was buried in a <u>grave</u> with gold and other <u>riches</u>. British archaeologists <u>found</u> the tomb and opened it. Inside was a <u>gorgeous</u> gold mask with the <u>king's</u> face on it.

5. old   _____

6. grave   _____

7. riches   _____

8. found   _____

9. gorgeous   _____

10. king's   _____

READING STRATEGY

Use with textbook pages 93.

Distinguishing Fact and Opinion

A **fact** is a statement that someone can prove because there is evidence. An **opinion** is the statement of a belief, which cannot be proved. To help you distinguish opinions from facts, look for words like *believe, think, feel, might,* and *perhaps.* To help you find facts, ask, "Can this statement be proved?"

Read each sentence below. Is it a fact or an opinion? Write *F* for *Fact* or *O* for *Opinion* in the space provided.

_____ **1.** For thousands of years, wind and sand have eroded the Sphinx.

_____ **2.** The Incas built Machu Picchu from about 1460 to 1470 c.e.

_____ **3.** In the early 1500s, everyone left the city, and no one knows why.

_____ **4.** Perhaps people died or left because of smallpox, a deadly disease that was brought by the Spanish.

_____ **5.** Ancient peoples built Stonehenge about 5,000 years ago.

_____ **6.** Perhaps Stonehenge was created to mark the rise of the sun and moon throughout the centuries.

_____ **7.** In 1922, a group led by British archaeologists Howard Carter and Lord Carnarvon opened the tomb of Tutankhamen.

_____ **8.** Lord Carnarvon died soon after opening the tomb.

_____ **9.** The famous Loch Ness monster may be a living dinosaur-like reptile called a plesiosaur.

_____ **10.** The first reports of Bigfoot date back to 1811.

Use with textbook pages 102–104.

Summary: "Truth or Lies?"

This passage presents three mysteries for readers to solve. In each mystery, a character tells part of the truth, but not the whole truth. Readers have to decide what is the truth and what is a lie.

Visual Summary

Half Truth	Whole Truth
A man in Trinidad explains his arrest by saying, "I picked up a rope I found on the ground."	The rope was attached to a cow he was stealing.
When Helen's mother finds only one cookie in the jar, Helen says, "I didn't touch one."	It's true Helen didn't touch one, but she touched—and ate—all the others.
A boy told his parents he got a hundred on his math and history tests.	He got a combined score of 100, a 60 on the math test and a 40 on the history test.

Use What You Know

Give an example of a TV commercial that uses language that makes what is not true seem true.

_____

_____

_____

_____

_____

Text Structure: Short Story

The events of a short story usually center around a problem called the conflict. Usually the story ends with a resolution, in which the conflict is settled. Circle the resolution of "Stolen Rope." Explain the conflict that it resolves.

MARK THE TEXT

_____

_____

_____

Reading Strategy: Distinguishing Fact and Opinion

A fact is something that can be proved. An opinion is an idea that someone believes is true but that cannot be proved. Underline a remark in "Stolen Rope" that expresses an opinion. What half truth led the person to have this opinion?

MARK THE TEXT

_____

_____

_____

Truth or Lies
by George Shannon
Stolen Rope

A man in Trinidad was being led through town on his way to jail. His hands were chained behind his back, and one of his ankles was chained to the officer who was leading him. As the two men neared the **village square**, a former neighbor of the arrested man passed by.

"What have you done that you're in chains and sentenced to jail?"

The chained man sighed. "I picked up a rope I found on the ground."

"You poor man!" said the neighbor. "There's more **injustice** in the **courts** than I realized."

"I know. It's terrible. Please tell them to set me free."

The man being taken to jail had spoken the **truth**, but he was also far from **innocent**.

What is the truth, the whole truth?
And where's the lie?

The Whole Truth

While it was true that the thief was being **punished** for picking up a rope, he was lying by what he did *not* say. The rope he picked up was tied to a cow.

---

village square, central part of a village
injustice, not being treated fairly
courts, places where someone is asked about a crime
truth, what is true; the correct facts
innocent, not guilty of doing something wrong
punished, made to suffer because of doing something wrong

The Cookie Jar

Helen's mother had finished baking a **batch** of cookies when a neighbor came over and asked for help.

"I'll just be gone a few minutes," said her mother as she put the cookies into the cookie jar. "No snacking while I'm next door. These are for the party tonight."

When Helen's mother returned and checked the cookie jar, there was only one cookie left.

"Helen!" she called as she stomped upstairs. "I told you *not* to eat those cookies I made for the party tonight."

"I didn't touch one," said Helen.

"Well, they sure didn't fly away **on their own**! You can stay in your room till you decide to tell the truth."

What's the truth, the whole truth?
And where's the lie?

The Whole Truth

Helen's exact words, "I didn't touch one," were true. She had not touched *one* cookie, the only one she'd left in the jar uneaten. She had, however, touched—and eaten—all the rest.

---

batch, group of things
on their own, by themselves

Comprehension Check

For what event does Helen's mother bake cookies? Circle the event. Does it seem likely Helen will attend the event? Why or why not? **MARK THE TEXT**

_____

_____

_____

Reading Strategy: Noting Causes and Effects

Why does the mother leave the cookies alone with Helen? Underline the cause. Why do you think Helen eats the cookies when her mother asks her not to? **MARK THE TEXT**

_____

_____

_____

Text Structure: Short Story

Remember, a short story usually is about a struggle or problem called the conflict. The conflict is usually settled, one way or the other, in a section called the resolution at the end. Explain the conflict and resolution in "The Cookie Jar."

_____

_____

_____

_____

School Days

A boy came running into the house for a snack after school and gave his mother a hug.

"How was your day?" asked his mother.

The boy grinned. "I got **a hundred** on my math and history tests!"

"That's wonderful," said his mother. "We'll celebrate with a special supper tonight."

It was a delicious meal, but when **report cards** came the next week, the boy's mother discovered there had been nothing to celebrate after all.

"How could you get an F in history and a D in math when you didn't miss anything on your tests last week? Did they catch you **cheating**? I certainly hope you weren't telling me **lies**!"

"Oh, no," answered the boy. "I'd never cheat. And as sure as I didn't cheat, I told you the truth."

His mother **grumbled** and frowned. "Well, something's not what it seems to be. I'm sure of that."

What's the truth, the whole truth?
And where's the lie?

The Whole Truth

The boy had gotten a hundred on his math and history tests. But it was a **combined score** of 100 for both tests—a 60 on the math test and a 40 on the history test.

---

a **hundred**, 100—perfect score
report cards, documents giving a student's grades
cheating, doing something that is not honest
lies, things that are not true
grumbled, complained in a quiet but angry way
combined score, total amount

Comprehension Check

Circle the letter grades that the boy gets in history and math on his report card. Why does his mother decide he was lying when he said he got 100 on his math and history tests?

_____

_____

_____

Text Structure: Short Story

A mystery is a story in which the whole truth is not revealed until the end. Would you say these three stories are mysteries? Why or why not?

_____

_____

_____

Reading Strategy: Distinguishing Fact and Opinion

Remember, a fact is something that can be proved. An opinion is an idea that someone believes is true but that cannot be proved. Underline an opinion stated by a character in this story. Explain how a misleading fact causes the character to state this opinion.

_____

_____

_____

Retell It!

Retell one of the last two stories in the form of a short riddle, with an answer. Follow this example for the first story: "How can a person be accused of stealing a cow when he just picked up a rope?" *(Answer: There was a cow—that didn't belong to the person—tied to the rope.)* The riddle might start "When is a person . . . ?" or "How can a person . . . ?"

_____

_____

_____

_____

_____

Reader's Response

What was your opinion of the three characters who told half truths? Explain your reactions.

_____

_____

_____

_____

_____

_____

_____

Think About the Skill

How did distinguishing facts and opinions help you understand the stories?

_____

_____

_____

_____

_____

Name _____ Date _____

GRAMMAR

Use with textbook page 106.

The Present Progressive

The **present progressive** describes an action that is happening now. The present progressive uses a form of *be* with a verb + *-ing*. Here is an example: *The Winstons are traveling to Egypt.*

When the verb ends in *-e*, drop the *-e* before adding *-ing*, as in these examples:

> rake ➤ raking   rise ➤ rising

When the verb ends in a vowel and a consonant, double the final consonant before adding *-ing*, as in these examples:

> stop ➤ stopping   slam ➤ slamming

Read the eyewitness account. For each verb (in parentheses), write the present progressive form of the verb on the lines below. The first one has been done for you.

Hello. This is Wanda Wilson. Welcome to *Weird and Wild World*. Today, we (visit) Tibet. Our team (search) for the legendary
1   2
yeti. We (hope) to find one. I (feel) very optimistic. Everyone
3   4
(talk) about the yeti.
5

Wait. I (get) a message from one of our reporters. Let's go to
6
our camera.

Our camera (point) at a cave. A strange creature (come) out of
7   8
the cave! Is it a yeti? It (look) right at us!
9

[*Several moments later.*] Never mind. It is just another news reporter with another large camera. He (wait) for a yeti, too.
10

1. __*are visiting*__   6. _____

2. _____   7. _____

3. _____   8. _____

4. _____   9. _____

5. _____   10. _____

GRAMMAR

Use after the lesson about adjective placement in compound sentences.

Adjective Placement in Compound Sentences

A compound sentence combines two simple sentences. A conjunction such as *and*, *but*, or *or* joins the sentences. A **comma** comes before the conjunction.

Adjectives can appear in either part of a compound sentence. An adjective before the comma describes a noun or pronoun before the comma. An adjective after the comma describes a noun or pronoun in that part of the sentence.

<u>Mysteries</u> are <u>exciting</u>, and the <u>Loch Ness Monster</u> is very <u>mysterious</u>.

Exciting describes *mysteries.*   *Mysterious* describes *Loch Ness Monster.*

Circle the adjectives in each sentence. Draw a line to show the word or words they describe.

1. Machu Picchu is old, but the Pyramids are really ancient.

2. The strange statue is called the Sphinx, and curious scientists still study it today.

3. The researchers find broken pieces, but they build a complete model.

4. Stonehenge is built of heavy stones, but the strange monument can still be damaged.

5. Easter Island is tiny, and it is covered with huge statues.

6. Howard Carter opened an ancient tomb, and he made a great discovery.

7. King Tutankhamen's mask is blue and gold, and it is also beautiful.

8. The Loch Ness monster might not be real, but the creature certainly is mysterious.

9. Giant squids may have long tentacles, but they can't crush large ships.

10. Bigfoot is supposed to be large and hairy, and he leaves huge footprints.

SKILLS FOR WRITING

Use with textbook page 107.

Using Prepositional Phrases

Some prepositions show place—where people or things are located. A **prepositional phrase** is a preposition + a noun or pronoun. Noticing prepositional phrases will help you better understand what you read.

Read the sentences below. Underline the preposition(s) that show place in each sentence.

1. There are three stars in Orion's Belt.

2. Was the Sphinx once buried under the sea?

3. The moon was behind the pyramids.

4. Machu Picchu was an ancient city in the Andes Mountains.

5. Stonehenge is a mysterious monument in England.

6. Easter Island is a tiny island in the Pacific Ocean.

7. Tutankhamen was a pharaoh in ancient Egypt.

8. The Loch Ness monster was reported to be seen near the lake.

9. Many people in the United States claim to have seen Bigfoot.

10. Easter Island is located off Chile's coast.

PROOFREADING AND EDITING

Use with textbook page 108.

Read the text carefully. Find all the mistakes. Look for errors using present progressive and prepositional phrases. Rewrite the text correctly on the lines below.

A Curious Museum

Jerome is at his bedroom. He are creating his own Museum of Mysteries, and he is hope to share it with other people. Right now, he is make a sculpture of a pyramid.

His room is begining to look like a real museum! One display shows the pyramids at Giza is Egypt. Next to the pyramids is a model of the Loch Ness monster swiming across a lake. Two drawings of big, hairy creatures is hanging on the wall. One shows Bigfoot in the forest, and the other shows a yeti climbing a snow-capped mountain

Jerome is planning to finish his museum by next saturday. He is inviting his friends and neighbors. Everyone will enjoy the strange things in Jerome's Museum of Mysteries. He is planning to take pictures and to write a magazine article about his museum.

_____

_____

_____

_____

_____

_____

_____

_____

_____

_____

_____

SPELLING

Use after the spelling lesson.

Adding -ing to Verbs

Read the list of verbs from the selections. Add -ing to each verb and write it on the line. Then show that you know the spelling rule by listing each in the correct column of the chart.

1. bake _____

2. lead _____

3. run _____

4. cheat _____

5. explore _____

6. finish _____

7. swim _____

8. grin _____

9. use _____

10. move _____

Just Add -ing	Drop Silent -e Before Adding -ing	Double the Final Consonant Letter Before Adding -ing

UNIT 3 Mysterious Ways

PART 2

Contents

VOCABULARY

Use with textbook page 111.

Read the words in the box. Then read each pair of sentences below. Choose a word or phrase from the box to complete the second sentence. Write it in the space provided.

> guilty   case   phony   evidence   up to mischief

1. The boys in the park ran when the security guard approached. This made the security

   guard think that the boys were _____ .

2. In the movie, the woman in the uniform was not a real security guard. She was

   wearing a security guard's clothes but was a _____ .

3. There was a tire track left in the mud at the scene of the crime. A picture of the tire

   track was used as _____ in court.

4. The detectives put all the clues together. Once again, they were able to solve a

   difficult _____ .

5. The movie kept the audience wondering who was _____ of

   the crime.

Read the clues. Use the words in the box to complete the crossword puzzle. (Hint: You will not use all the words.)

> | crime | phony | solution | evidence |
> | solved | tools | case | guilty |

ACROSS
3. answer to a problem
4. information used to prove something
5. not innocent

DOWN
1. something a detective tries to solve
2. false or fake

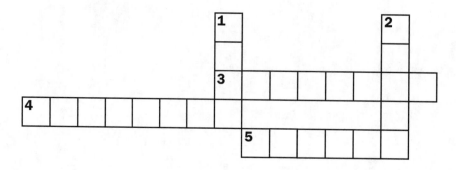

VOCABULARY BUILDING

Understanding Antonyms
Antonyms are words that mean the opposite of each other. Read the pairs of antonyms in the chart. You can also find antonyms for words in a dictionary.

Antonyms			
old	new	dry	wet
hot	cold	tall	short
quick	slow	before	after
early	late	full	empty
front	back	always	never

Read the sentences. Write an antonym for the underlined word in the space provided. Use the chart above to help you.

1. Max noticed a <u>tall</u> man with a briefcase walking toward him. _____

2. Max did not want to be <u>late</u>. _____

3. Miss Fritz was the <u>oldest</u> music teacher at Harborville. _____

4. Jenny, Brittany, and Mitzi were <u>always</u> together. _____

5. Brittany's ankle felt okay as long as she moved <u>slowly</u>. _____

6. Somebody touched the cement while it was still <u>wet</u>. _____

7. Nina was eating <u>cold</u> pizza for lunch. _____

8. Mrs. Decker's glass of lemonade was <u>full</u>. _____

9. You can put a lot of things in the <u>back</u> of a truck. _____

10. The man wanted to see the house <u>before</u> it was sold. _____

READING STRATEGY

Use with textbook page 111.

Using a Graphic Organizer to Compare and Contrast Texts

When you **compare**, you notice how things are alike. When you **contrast**, you identify how things are different. A graphic organizer can help you compare and contrast when you read.

After you finish reading the stories, think of how they are alike and how they are different. Then fill in the chart below.

	The Case of the Surprise Visitor	The Case of the Defaced Sidewalk	The Case of the Disappearing Signs
What was the mystery?	1.	2.	3.
Who solved the mystery?	4.	5.	6.
What clues helped the detective solve the mystery?	7.	8.	9.

10. Which mystery did you think was the easiest to solve? Why? _____

_____

_____

_____

_____

_____

_____

Use with textbook pages 120–122.

Summary: "How to Make a Friend Disappear" and "Water Trick"

These science experiments show how you can use science to have fun creating a mystery. The first experiment tells how to use a mirror to make a friend disappear. The second experiment tells how to keep water inside a glass, even when the glass is turned upside down.

Visual Summary

Two Tricks	
Name of Trick	**What the Trick Does**
How to Make a Friend Disappear	Uses a mirror to make it seem like someone disappears.
Water Trick	Keeps water inside a glass that is turned upside down.

List three tricks you have heard about or seen a magician perform.

1._____

2._____

3._____

A description of a science experiment includes the things used in the experiment and the steps taken to perform the experiment. Under what two headings is this information given in "How to Make a Friend Disappear"? Underline the two headings. How many steps does it take to perform the experiment?

MARK THE TEXT

_____

How to Make a Friend Disappear

Materials

• two chairs

• a small mirror

Method

1. Sit on a chair with a wall to your right. Ask your partner to sit **opposite** you. Your partner should sit very **still**.

2. Hold the bottom of the mirror with your left hand. Put the edge of the mirror against the side of your nose. The **reflecting surface** should face the wall. Don't move your hand.

3. Turn the mirror so that your right eye sees only the reflection of the wall. Your left eye should look straight ahead at your partner.

4. Move your right hand in front of the wall like you are **erasing** a chalkboard. Watch as parts of your friend's face disappear!

Magicians use this trick to make objects "disappear." They use mirrors to hide the objects from view.

Some people see this effect more easily than others. A few people never see it. You may have to try it several times. Don't **give up**!

_____

materials, things you need
method, instructions, way to do something
opposite, facing; across from
still, without moving
reflecting surface, side of the mirror where you can see yourself
erasing, removing something
give up, stop trying

If you don't see your friend's face disappear, one of your eyes might be stronger than the other. Try the experiment again. This time, change the eye you use to look at the person and the eye you use to look at the wall.

Why Is It So?

Usually, your two eyes see slightly different pictures of the world around you. Your brain combines these two pictures to create a single image.

In this experiment, the mirror lets your eyes see two very different views. One eye looks straight ahead at your partner, while the other eye looks at the wall and your moving hand. Your brain tries to put together a picture that makes sense by choosing parts of both views.

Reading Strategy: Noting Causes and Effects

Why might the trick not work for some people? Underline the cause. How do you think those people would react if they were in the audience watching the trick being performed?

_____

_____

_____

_____

_____

Text Structure: Science Experiment

Circle the heading under which the trick is explained.

Comprehension Check

Underline what your two eyes normally see and what the brain then does to help you see the whole picture. How does the mirror change the situation?

_____

_____

_____

_____

_____

_____

Choose one and complete it.
1. Draw pictures showing the steps of one of the experiments (the one on pages 120–121 or the one on page 122).
2. Do research on the Internet to learn more about molecules and how they work. Take notes on what you find.
3. Imagine that you will perform one of the experiments as a trick for an audience. What music or sound effects might you use in the background? What visual effects might you use? List your ideas.

Water Trick

Materials
- a drinking glass
- a handkerchief
- a rubber band

Method
1. Fill a glass three-quarters full with water.
2. Place a **damp** handkerchief over the top of it.
3. Place a rubber band around the rim of the glass so that it is holding the handkerchief.
4. Push down on the center of the handkerchief until it touches the water. Make sure the rubber band stays around the glass.
5. Keep your fingers pressed on the handkerchief and turn the glass upside down. The water will remain in the glass.
6. Pull the handkerchief tight, still keeping the rubber band on, so that the curved shape disappears. The water will remain in the glass.

Why Is It So?

Molecules at the surface of water attract each other and **clump together**. This is called surface tension. Surface tension prevents the molecules from passing through the small holes of the handkerchief.

At home you can look at different liquids and see how much or how little surface tension they have. Put a drop of water onto a plate and it will form a rounded ball. This is because of surface tension. Other substances have more or less surface tension. Put a drop of vinegar onto a plate and on a different plate put a drop of oil. Can you tell which liquid has more or less surface tension?

---

handkerchief, square piece of cloth
damp, a little wet
molecules, the smallest parts of something; they can't be seen with the eye
clump together, form a group or mass

Retell It!

Imagine that you are explaining one of these experiments to a young child. What tone of voice will you use? What changes would you make in the words you use? List your ideas.

_____

_____

_____

_____

_____

Reader's Response

How would you react if you saw one of these tricks performed?

_____

_____

_____

_____

_____

_____

Think About the Skill

How did examining cause-and-effect relationships help you understand this experiment?

_____

_____

_____

_____

_____

_____

_____

GRAMMAR

Use with textbook page 124.

Imperatives

An **imperative** gives an order, an instruction, or a direction. In sentences with an imperative, the subject is not stated. It is understood to be *you*. Imperative sentences end with a period or an exclamation point.

(You) Follow these directions.
       Look in the mirror.
       Turn the mirror sideways.
       Watch what happens!

Read these directions for making your own refrigerator. Then complete the list of instructions by writing the missing imperative sentences in order. Circle the verb in each sentence. Follow the examples.

A Cool Trick

Make your own refrigerator! All you need is a clay pot, some water, a cold can of soda, and a stone.

Start with a clay pot. Soak the pot in water. Turn the pot upside down. Place the pot over your can of soda. Is there a hole at the bottom of your pot? Cover the hole with a stone.

The soda will stay cool. Why? As the water disappears, it takes heat away. The can under the pot stays cool. Try this experiment at home. Watch what happens when the pot dries out.

(Start) with a clay pot.

1. _____

2. _____

3. _____

(Cover) the hole with a stone.

4. _____

5. _____

Name _____ Date _____

GRAMMAR

Use after the lesson about end punctuation.

Punctuation: Periods and Exclamation Points
A declarative sentence makes a statement. It ends with a **period (.)**.
An exclamatory sentence expresses excitement. It ends with an
exclamation point (!).

Answer each question with a complete sentence in the space provided.
Use the end punctuation shown. If the end punctuation is an exclamation
point, be sure to write an answer that expresses excitement.

1. How do you feel about reading suspenseful mysteries?

   _____!

2. Are you good at solving mysteries?

   _____.

3. If someone solved a mystery for you, what would you say?

   _____!

4. Have you ever met a real detective?

   _____.

5. What are some skills of a good detective?

   _____.

6. In the mirror trick, why did the person's face disappear?

   _____.

7. What would you say about an amazing trick that puzzled you?

   _____!

8. Did you see the girl or the old woman first when you looked at the picture on
   page 121 of your textbook?

   _____.

9. What did you think when water did not pour out of the upside-down glass?

   _____!

10. What is surface tension?

   _____.

SKILLS FOR WRITING

Use with textbook page 125.

Writing Clues

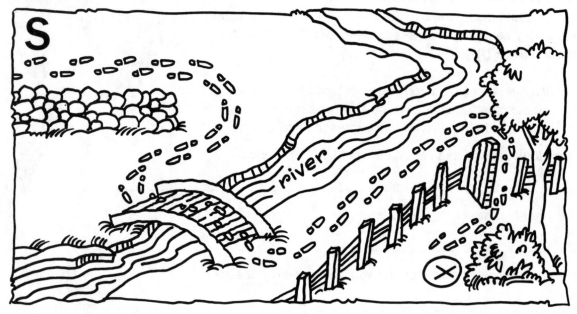

Find the treasure! Use this map to help you write the clues below in the correct order.
Circle the imperative verb or verbs. The first one has been done for you.

Walk to the fence.	At the end of the wall, turn right.
Walk toward the bridge.	Then cross the bridge.
Dig under the bush.	Turn left and follow along the fence.
Go through the gate.	Follow along the stone wall.
Open the gate.	Start at the S.

1. _(Start) at the S._ _____

2. _____

3. _____

4. _____

5. _____

6. _____

7. _____

8. _____

9. _____

10. _____

PROOFREADING AND EDITING

Use with textbook page 126.

Read these clues for a treasure hunt carefully. Find all the mistakes. Make sure imperative sentences use correct verb forms. Rewrite the composition correctly on the lines below.

Internet Mystery Hunt

I found some great mysterys! Would you like to know how. You can find many cool facts on the Internet. Just turning on your computer and go online!

First, go to your favorate search engine Types in words that describe what you are searching for. look at photos of the Loch Ness monster. They may look real, but they're probably phoney. Learn more about Bigfoot, too. Be sure to check out the latest pictures of giant squids. They are amazeing! Print out the pages that interesting you so that you can share what you learn with your class.

_____

_____

_____

_____

_____

_____

_____

_____

_____

_____

_____

_____

_____

_____

SPELLING

Use after the spelling lesson.

Number Words

The **number words** for the numbers 1 to 12 do not follow a spelling pattern.
Write the number word for the number in parentheses ( ) in the space provided. Use a dictionary if necessary.

1.   (8) _____   6.   (2) _____

2.   (1) _____   7.   (4) _____

3.   (7) _____   8.   (10) _____

4.   (11) _____   9.   (3) _____

5.   (12) _____   10.   (6) _____

The **number words** from 13 to 19 end with *teen*. Write the number word for the number in parentheses ( ) in the space provided.

11.   (15) _____

12.   (13) _____

13.   (19) _____

14.   (17) _____

15.   (18) _____

The **number words** for 21 to 29 begin with *twenty* + a hyphen (-). Numbers from 30 to 99 follow the same pattern as numbers in the 20s. Circle the correct spelling of each number below.

16.   38   thirtyeight   three-eight   thirty-eight

17.   24   twenty-four   twenty four   two-four

18.   77   seventyseven   seventy-seven   seven-seven

19.   46   four-six   fortysix   forty-six

20.   52   fifty-two   five-two   fifty two

UNIT 4 Conflict

PART 1

Contents

Name _____ Date _____

Use with textbook page 137.

Read the sentences. Then write one of the words in **boldfaced** type on each numbered line below to complete the incomplete sentences.

The **terrorists** caused much fear when they unexpectedly attacked.

During a war, the side you are fighting against is your **enemy**.

Countries that are **allies** work together to defeat their enemy.

The losing country **surrendered** when they could no longer fight.

The war ended when all sides signed a formal **treaty**, agreeing to its terms.

The three countries that joined together to win the war were _____.
1

They fought together to defeat their _____. Even before war was
2

declared, some _____ had attacked and caught their victims by
3

surprise. Finally, the countries that were losing the war _____
4

to the others. After the war, some countries honored the _____, but
5

some did not.

Read the clues. Use words in the box to complete the crossword puzzle. Use a dictionary. (Hint: You will not use all of the words.)

| allies   assassinate   enemy   soldier   treaty   surrendered   tanks   tension |

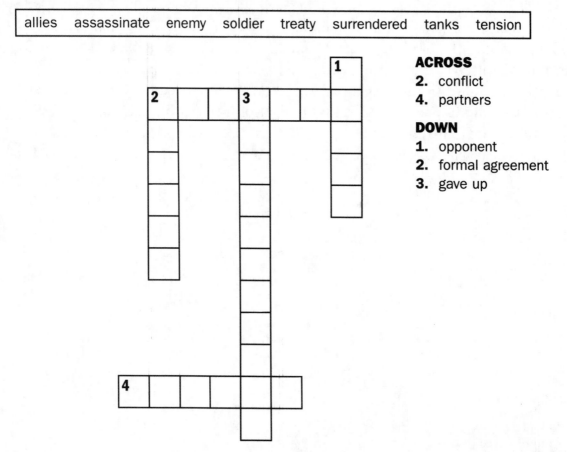

ACROSS
2. conflict
4. partners

DOWN
1. opponent
2. formal agreement
3. gave up

VOCABULARY BUILDING

Understanding Phrasal Verbs

A **phrasal verb** is a two- or three-word verb. It contains the main verb and at least one preposition. *Get up* and *look forward to* are phrasal verbs. The meaning of a phrasal verb is different from the meaning of the verb alone (*get* or *look*).

Complete each sentence with a phrasal verb from the chart. Remember that some phrasal verbs can be separated.

Verbs that can be separated		Verbs that cannot be separated	
verb	meaning	verb	meaning
brought on	caused	took care of	to protect, provide for
gave up	stopped fighting	look forward to	glad to see in the future
broken up	made into smaller units	get over	to forget hurt or pain
		get along with	doing without conflict

1. Destruction and loss of life _____ _____ the defeat of the suffering country.

2. The weakened troops _____ the fight _____ and surrendered.

3. The weary soldiers were _____ _____ into smaller groups and led away.

4. The doctors and nurses _____ _____ _____ the wounded.

5. Peace was won and now countries could _____ _____

    _____ the future.

6. It would be hard for some soldiers to _____ _____ their memories of war.

7. If countries could _____ _____ _____ one another, there would be no war.

Read the phrasal verb and its meaning in parentheses ( ). Use the phrasal verb in a sentence.

8. (take off—remove something) _____

9. (go on—continue) _____

10. (pulled out—left) _____

READING STRATEGY

Use with textbook page 137.

Noting Causes and Effects

A history text is often organized by **cause** and **effect** to show relationships among events. A **cause** is what makes something happen, or the reason something happens. The **effect** is what happens, the result of the cause. Words that signal cause/effect relationships include: *because, so, therefore, when, as a result, since, first, then,* and *for that reason.*

Here are some examples:

- The cause/effect relationship may be stated in separate sentences.
  Example: *First*, great tensions built up among countries. *Then* they went to war.
                                     cause   effect
- The cause/effect relationship may be stated in one sentence.
  Example: *Because* great tensions built up, the nations went to war.
                       cause   effect
- Even though it happened later, the effect may be stated before the cause.
  Example: The nations went to war *because* great tensions built up.
              effect   cause

Read the sentences. Label the cause and the effect in each. Next, circle the word or words that signal a cause/effect relationship.

                             cause   effect
Example: (Because) each country wanted more power, the balance was easily upset.

1. Since Britain, France, and Germany traded with other countries, they had become competitive with each other.

2. Germany had bigger, more modern factories. As a result, Britain was worried.

3. Germany was worried because France had become powerful in Africa.

4. Russia and Austria wanted more power, so they were active in the Balkan states.

5. Finally two powerful alliances were formed because of the buildup of conflicts.

Use with textbook pages 146–148.

Summary: "Letter Home," "Can We Forget?" and "Grass"

"Letter Home" was written by a young British soldier in World War I. "Can We Forget?" and "Grass" are two poems about war. The three selections give different views of war and how it affects different people—the soldiers themselves, their loved ones, and people not directly affected by the war. It shows that soldiers face death in battle, that relatives suffer when they lose or worry about loved ones in battle, and that, in time, many people forget the suffering.

Visual Summary

Title	Who is the writer or speaker?	What is his or her main message?
"Letter Home"	Frank, a soldier in World War I	Though I know I may die at any time, I am not afraid and ask only that you pray for me.
"Can We Forget?"	the mother of a soldier	Can I ever forget the horror that my soldier son faced in war and my own fears and grief?
"Grass"	the grass at several battlefield cemeteries where soldiers killed in battle are buried	After many die in war, I cover up the battlefield cemeteries so that, in time, people forget the details and raw feelings of the war.

Name _____ Date _____

Letter Home

Use What You Know

List three things you know about soldiers in war.

1. _____

2. _____

3. _____

Text Structure: Letter

A personal letter usually provides information about the feelings of the person writing it. Underline words that show Frank's feelings toward his family. Sum up Frank's feelings about the possibility of his death.

 MARK THE TEXT

_____

_____

_____

_____

_____

Reading Strategy: Noting Causes and Effects

What recent event helped cause Frank to realize he may die at any time? Circle the details about this event. What effect do you think receiving this letter had on his family after learning he had died the next day?

 MARK THE TEXT

_____

_____

_____

Sunday afternoon, 1st September, 1918

My dear Father,

It is a strange feeling to me but a very real one, that every letter now that I write home to you or to the little sisters may be the last that I shall write or you read. I do not want you to think that I am depressed; indeed on the contrary, I am very cheerful. But out here, in odd moments the realization comes to me of how close death is to us. A week ago I was talking with a man, a Catholic, from Preston, who had been out here for nearly four years, untouched. He was looking forward with certainty to going on leave soon. And now he is dead — killed in a moment during our last advance. Well, it was God's will.

I say this to you because I hope that you will realize, as I do, the possibility of the like happening to myself. I feel very glad myself that I can look the fact in the face without fear or misgiving. Much as I hope to live through it all for your sakes and my little sisters! I am quite prepared to give my life as so many have done before me. All I can do is put myself in God's hands for him to decide, and you and the little ones pray for me to the Sacred Heart and Our Lady.

Well, I have not much time left and I must end. With my dear love. Pray for me.

Your son,

Frank

---

on the contrary, it's the opposite
going on leave, having a rest from fighting
look the fact in the face, deal with the reality
misgiving, doubt

Name _____ Date _____

Can We Forget?

Can I ever forget? Can I ever forget?
Oh, God! Can I ever forget
My soldier boy's smile and the light in his eye,
With the army badge fresh on his sleeve—
The firm clasp of his hand and the warmth of his kiss
As he said, "Dear, be brave and don't grieve"?

Can I ever forget? Can I ever forget?
Oh, God! Can I ever forget
How the wealth of his spirit shone out of his face
When he knew we might see him no more,
While we watched his dear form where he stood on
        the deck
As the steamer pulled out from the shore?

Can I ever forget? Can I ever forget?
Oh, God! Can I ever forget
The long, weary days in the hospital ward,
The brow knot with pain and the face, wan and white,
The fever-racked frame and the hideous night—
The death at the left and the death at the right —
Oh, God! Can I ever forget?

Can I ever forget? Can I ever forget?
Oh, God! Can I ever forget
All the fierce storms that raged in the wild warfare's
        wake—
All the ways where my lad did his part—
Or the messages chill over the telegraph line,
Or the cold charge that went through his heart?

                    Cora Inez Keyes

----

steamer, ship
ward, patients' room
fever-racked, full of fever
fierce, wild
lad, boy

Text Structure: Poem

The speaker in a poem, may or may not be the poet. Underline a detail that suggests the speaker here is the soldier's mother. What do you think happened to the speaker's son?

_____

_____

_____

Comprehension Check

Circle the question that the speaker keeps repeating. What is the implied, or suggested, answer to this question? Why?

_____

_____

_____

_____

Literary Element: Rhyme

Words that rhyme have the same sound except for their beginning sounds. For example, *bird* and *word* rhyme. Underline at least four pairs of rhyming words in this poem. Where in the lines do the rhymes fall?

_____

Name _____   Date _____

Grass

Pile the bodies high at Austerlitz and Waterloo.

Shovel them under and let me work—

     I am the grass;

     I cover all.

And pile them high at Gettysburg

And pile them high at Ypres and Verdun.

Shovel them under and let me work.

Two years, ten years, and passengers ask the conductor:

     What place is this?

     Where are we now?

     I am the grass.

     Let me work.

        Carl Sandburg

Austerlitz, Waterloo, Gettysburg, Ypres, Verdun, places where
  battles were fought
shovel them under, bury them
conductor, the person on a train or bus who sells tickets and
  announces stops

Text Structure: Poem

Circle the word that tells the identity of the speaker in this poem. What "work" does the speaker perform, and where does it perform that "work"?  MARK THE TEXT

_____

_____

Reading Strategy: Noting Causes and Effects

Underline the questions the passengers ask the conductor, and MARK THE TEXT circle the number of years that have passed when they ask these questions. What do you think causes them to ask these questions? Write your answer below.

_____

_____

Comprehension Check

What does the poem suggest happens to people's views of a war over time? Does the poem suggest this is a good or bad thing? Explain your opinion.

_____

_____

_____

_____

_____

_____

Choose one and complete it.
1. Draw a picture of what you visualized in one of the readings. Did you picture Frank's family, the mother's brave young soldier, or the grassy area years later?
2. Based on their poems, what do you think Carl Sandburg might say to Cora Inez Keyes about remembering the suffering of war? Write your ideas for a dialogue between the two poets.
3. Read one of the poems out loud. What emotion will you try to convey? Where will you pause for emphasis? List your ideas.

Retell It!

Write a sympathy note for the death of one of the soldiers in these selections. Your note might be to a family member or someone else who knew the soldier well. Include a few sentences summing up how you feel about war in general and about what happened to the soldier.

_____

_____

_____

_____

_____

_____

Reader's Response

Choose one selection, and explain whether or not you agree with the view of war it expresses.

_____

_____

_____

_____

_____

_____

Think About the Skill

How did noting causes and effects help you better understand the selections?

_____

_____

_____

_____

_____

_____

GRAMMAR

Use with textbook page 150.

Using so as a Conjunction

The conjunction *so* means "as a result" when it connects two sentences. The first sentence shows the **cause**, or reason, for something, and the second sentence shows the **effect**, or result. Use a comma before *so* when it joins two sentences.

Match the cause sentences in the left column to the effect sentences in the right column. Write the letter of the correct response in the space provided. Then combine the sentences using *so* on the lines provided below. Remember to use commas.

_____ **1.** Submarines travel underwater.

_____ **2.** Soldiers needed to see over the tops of trenches.

_____ **3.** Armies used poisonous gases.

_____ **4.** Most of the fighting took place during the night.

_____ **5.** Armies used modern weapons during WWI.

a. Soldiers wore specially designed masks.

b. Historians call it "the first modern war."

c. They are difficult to see.

d. They used periscope rifles.

e. Soldiers slept during the day.

6. _____

_____

7. _____

_____

8. _____

_____

9. _____

_____

10. _____

_____

GRAMMAR

Use after the lesson about *wh-* questions.

Wh- Questions

Informational texts often answer questions that begin with *who, what, where, when,* and *why.*

When did World War I begin?   **Who** killed Archduke Ferdinand?

Where is Sarajevo?   **Why** did the United States enter the war

What happened there?

Read the questions and their answers. Use a question word from the box to complete each question. Write the word on the line.

Who	What	Where	When	Why

1. _____ are tanks difficult to attack? (They are covered with heavy armor.)

2. _____ kind of ships travel underwater? (Submarines travel underwater.)

3. _____ did soldiers fight? (Soldiers fought in trenches.)

4. _____ did most fighting take place? (Most fighting took place at night.)

5. _____ was the U.S. President in 1917? (Woodrow Wilson was president in 1917.)

Write five questions of your own about World War I. Use the question words provided.

6. Who _____

   _____?

7. What _____

   _____?

8. Where _____

   _____?

9. When _____

   _____?

10. Why _____

    _____?

SKILLS FOR WRITING

Use with textbook page 151.

Cause-and-Effect Organization in Writing

Read the tips for writing a text with **cause-and-effect organization** on page 151 in your textbook.

Reread Frank Earley's letter on page 146. Then summarize the letter by completing the five cause/effect sentences below. For each, use the logical cause/effect sentence from the box. Follow the example.

The other man was killed.	It might be the last one he would write.
He could return to his family.	He wanted them to know that he was not depressed.
They would realize it could happen to him.	He was looking forward to going on leave.

Example: Frank felt strange about writing a letter home because *it might be the*

last one he would write.

1. He told his family that he was cheerful *because* _____

_____

2. The man who was killed had been in the war for nearly four years, *so* _____

_____

3. Frank realized how close death was to him *because* _____

_____

4. He told his family about the other man's death, *so* _____

_____

5. Frank said he wanted to live through the war, *so* _____

_____

PROOFREADING AND EDITING

Use with textbook page 152.

Read this passage written using cause-and-effect organization. Find the mistakes. Look for errors in some of the cause and effect sentences. There are also errors in spelling, capitalization, and punctuation. Then rewrite the passage correctly on the lines below.

Wet trenches

we moved camp last week. Their were no trenches in the area, we had to dig them. It was hard work, and my arms are still very tried. One week latter, the trenches are already crowded and smelly.

because it rains all the time, the trenches are wet. We put down duckboards the ground is very muddy. Yesterday, the mud was very deep so my boot got stuck.

I hope the war is over soon so I want to come home.

_____

_____

_____

_____

_____

_____

_____

_____

_____

_____

_____

_____

_____

_____

SPELLING

Use after the spelling lesson.

Adding -ed

Add -ed to the base form of a regular verb to form the **past tense**.

want + ed	=	wanted	sign + ed	=	signed
support + ed	=	supported	end + ed	=	ended

If the verb ends in e, add just -d.

move + d	=	moved	prepare + d	=	prepared

Add -ed or -d to each verb.

1. ask _____ 　　 8. gain _____

2. kill _____ 　　 9. live _____

3. trade _____ 　 10. defeat _____

4. join _____ 　　 11. surrender _____

5. agree _____ 　 12. cause _____

6. charge _____ 　 13. clasp _____

7. happen _____ 　 14. hope _____

Complete each sentence with a verb in the past tense. Add -ed or -d to verbs in the box.

place	protect	starve	sign	start	use

15. World War I _____ in 1914.

16. Soldiers _____ many modern weapons.

17. People in Germany _____ because they could not get food.

18. Gas masks _____ soldiers from poison gases.

19. Soldiers _____ wood boards at the bottom of trenches.

20. Germany _____ an armistice in 1918.

UNIT 4 Conflict

PART 2

Contents

VOCABULARY

Use with textbook page 155.

Read and complete the sentences by circling the letter for the correct answer.

1. When the war ends, people hope to live in _____.

   a. peace   **b.** suffering   **c.** emotions

2. When many people are killed at one time, it is called a _____.

   a. surrender   **b.** massacre   **c.** negotiate

3. Sick and injured people are taken to the hospital in an _____.

   a. emergency   **b.** emotions   **c.** ambulance

4. Violent conflicts, like war, often lead to great _____.

   a. suffering   **b.** negotiate   **c.** massacre

5. In order to solve a conflict, the two sides can _____ terms for peace.

   a. peace   **b.** negotiate   **c.** massacre

Read the clues. Then use words from the box to complete the crossword puzzle. (Hint: You will not use all of the words.)

ambulance	Sarajevo	emotion	massacre	peace
suffering	relatives	madness	negotiate	attic

ACROSS
2. mass murder
4. opposite of war

DOWN
1. talk to solve a conflict
2. insanity; chaos
3. vehicle that carries people to a hospital

VOCABULARY BUILDING

Understanding Collocations

Collocations are words that commonly appear together and form an expression.
Learning collocations can help you speak more naturally and understand more commonly
used expressions.

Example: Best friends are often separated in wartime.

Look at this chart of common collocations.

birthday present	go crazy
do my (or other pronoun) best	play cards
come home	keep warm
stay home	lose weight
best friend	make peace

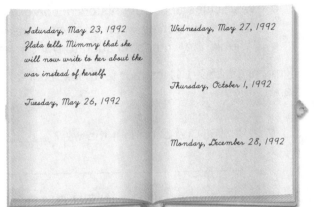

Use words from the chart to help you find
and circle the collocation in each sentence.

1. Zlata's best friend Mirna had a birthday
   soon after she left Sarajevo.

2. Zlata couldn't give Mirna her birthday present.

3. Zlata worries that she might go crazy from the war.

4. She hopes that the enemies will make peace.

5. In the meantime, she must do her best to go on.

6. Zlata's mother had lost weight.

7. Zlata wants to play cards with her parents.

8. It was hard to keep warm.

9. Zlata did not stay home.

10. They were worried that Mother hadn't come home.

READING STRATEGY

Use with textbook page 155.

Analyzing Historical Context

Personal narratives, such as diaries, letters, and journals, let readers get to know the person who wrote them. Knowing the **historical context** of the time in which the narrative was written makes the text more understandable and meaningful. As you read personal narratives, think about the historical context.

- What clues about the historical context do you get from skimming the pages?
- What is happening when and where the writer is writing?
- What is the writer's reaction to what is happening?

Skim pages 156–161 of your textbook. Look at the pictures, captions, and dates of the diary entries.

1. What do you find out about the war? _____

_____

2. What clues do you find about Zlata's daily life? _____

3. What is the time-period covered in the diary? _____

4. Read the introduction on page 156. What do you learn about Zlata that you had

   not already figured out? _____

5. Read "About the Author" on page 161. Did Zlata survive the war? _____

6. In her first entry, dated Saturday, May 23, what does Zlata say she is writing about?

_____

Read the diary entries with the following dates. Describe what is happening in the Bosnian War and Zlata's reactions.

Dates	What is happening	Zlata's reactions
Tuesday, May 26	7.	8.
Wednesday, May 27	9.	10.

Use with textbook pages 164–166.

Summary: "The Physical World: The Balkans"

This passage tells about the Balkans, a group of countries in southeast Europe. It describes the land and the people in the Balkans and explains why this area has had many wars.

Visual Summary

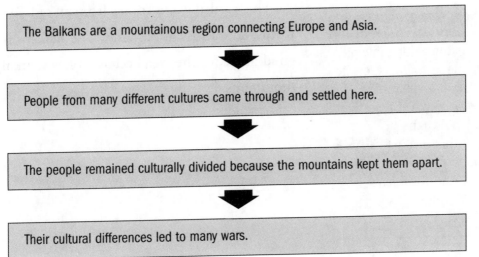

The Balkans are a mountainous region connecting Europe and Asia.

People from many different cultures came through and settled here.

The people remained culturally divided because the mountains kept them apart.

Their cultural differences led to many wars.

Name _____ Date _____

The Physical World: The Balkans

The Balkans are a group of countries in southeast Europe. Slovenia, Croatia, Bosnia and Herzegovina, Macedonia, Albania, Greece, Bulgaria, Romania, Serbia, Montenegro, and part of Turkey are all in the Balkans.

The word *Balkans* comes from an old Turkish word that means "mountains." The Balkans is a good name for the area because it has so many mountains.

Use What You Know

List three things you know or would like to know about Eastern Europe.

1. _____

2. _____

3. _____

Text Structure: Informational Text

Informational text is writing in which the main purpose is to give facts to the reader. Often it explains the meanings of new terms. Circle the term (in *italic* type) that is explained on this page. What does the term mean, and to which countries does it refer?

MARK THE TEXT

_____

_____

_____

_____

_____

_____

_____

Reading Strategy: Distinguishing Fact and Opinion

A fact is something that can be proved. An opinion is an idea that someone believes is true but that cannot be proved. Most of the sentences on this page provide facts. Underline the one opinion that is included.

MARK THE TEXT

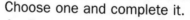

Choose one and complete it.
1. Do an interview with someone from a Balkan country. Use the information you just read for questions and answers.
2. Do research about one of the different countries that make up the Balkans.

104

Unit 4 Conflict Part 2

The Balkans form a land bridge between Europe and Asia. Since ancient times, this area has been the border between the empires of the East and the West. People from different **ethnic** groups traveled through the region and settled in the hills and valleys of the region. The mountains made it difficult for the different groups of people to **interact** with each other. Therefore, many different languages, cultures, and customs developed. These differences have led to many conflicts in the area. The Balkans are often called "the **powder keg** of Europe" because many wars have started there.

---

ethnic, cultural
interact, communicate, do things together
powder keg, something that is ready to blow up at any time

Choose one and complete it.
1. Do research to find out about one war in the Balkans. What changes happened because of the war?
2. Find out about the different cultures and customs of people in the Balkans. Use the Internet. Choose one custom that interests you. Create a magazine feature about the custom. Draw a picture and write a caption for it.

Comprehension Check

Underline the words that tell what the Balkans connect.
Why do the Balkans have so many different ethnic groups?

_____

_____

_____

Literary Element: Images

Images are words or phrases that help create pictures in a reader's mind. Circle images that help readers picture the Balkans.
What image helps you picture the Balkans' role in history? Write the words and explain how they help you on the lines below.

_____

_____

_____

Reading Strategy: Distinguishing Fact and Opinion

Underline the sentence that tells what the Balkans' ethnic differences led to. Does the sentence state a fact or an opinion? Explain your answer.

_____

_____

_____

_____

Text Structure: Informational Text

Underline the information about the languages  **MARK THE TEXT** spoken in the Balkans. What problems do you think so many languages in a fairly small area might create? Write your ideas on the lines below.

_____

_____

_____

_____

Reading Strategy: Distinguishing Fact and Opinion

Circle a word in the last paragraph that expresses an opinion about the Balkans. What could **MARK THE TEXT** the writer do to support this opinion?

_____

_____

_____

_____

Literary Element: Images

Underline an image that helps you better understand the effects of war in the Balkans. Explain what this image suggests about the **MARK THE TEXT** kinds of effects that war has had in the region.

_____

_____

The two main religions in the Balkans are Christianity and Islam. The people of the Balkans speak many different languages: Albanian, Greek, Serbian, Croatian, Hungarian, Macedonian, Turkish, Slovenian, Bulgarian, and Romanian.

The Balkans are a land of many contrasts. They have ancient and modern cities and beautiful mountains and rivers, as well as the scars of war.

Choose one and complete it.
1. Draw a map of the Balkans. Include the names of all the countries and the bodies of water nearby. Use an atlas or the Internet to get your information.
2. Do research on the Internet to find out more about the languages spoken in the Balkans. Take notes on what you find.
3. Create a pantomime or ballet based on the history of the Balkans. List the events and ideas you want to show, and explain what you and other performers will do to show those events and ideas.

Retell It!

Imagine you are a TV newscaster. The Balkans are in the news again, and you have to explain what they are. Which key details from the selection would you include? List those key details.

_____

_____

_____

_____

_____

_____

_____

_____

_____

Reader's Response

What would you suggest to help curb warfare in the Balkans?

_____

_____

_____

_____

Think About the Skill

How did distinguishing fact from opinion help you with this selection?

_____

_____

_____

_____

_____

GRAMMAR

Use with textbook page 168.

Using Pronoun Referents

Pronouns replace nouns. There are two types of pronouns: **subject** and **object** pronouns. Subject pronouns replace nouns that are subjects. They usually come before the verb.

> **Example: Zlata** writes in her diary everyday.   **She** writes about the day's events.

Object pronouns replace nouns that come after the verb.
> **Example:** Zlata misses **Mirna**.   Zlata makes **her** a present.

She refers to Zlata. The word *her* refers to Mirna. *She* and *her* are **pronoun referents**. Singular pronouns refer to singular nouns. Plural pronouns refer to plural nouns.

Read each pair of sentences from *Zlata's Diary*. In the second sentence, circle the pronoun that is the referent for the underlined noun or nouns in the first sentence. The first one has been done for you.

1. Almost all my friends have left. Even if (they) were here, who knows whether we'd be able to see one another.

2. I was so unhappy because of that war in Dubrovnik. I never dreamed it would move to Sarajevo.

3. I keep thinking about Mirna. I would love to see her so much.

4. Daddy and I were tearing our hair out. We didn't know what had happened to her.

5. I look at Daddy. He really has lost a lot of weight.

6. This stupid war is destroying my childhood. It is destroying my parents' lives.

7. Mommy and Daddy are so unhappy now. I'm going to play a game of cards with them.

8. My piano teacher and I kissed and hugged. We hadn't seen each other since March.

9. Mirna's grandparents had to leave their apartment. It was shelled.

10. My dear Mimmy, Mommy and Daddy are thinking about something. As I write to you, I wonder what they are thinking about.

GRAMMAR

Use after the lesson about possessives with apostrophes.

Possessives with Apostrophes
A **possessive** shows that something belongs to someone or something. Use an **apostrophe** (') and s to form most possessives.

To form the possessive of a singular noun, add an apostrophe and s ('s).
the diary that belongs to Zlata   Zlata's diary
the teacher that belongs to the class   the class's teacher

To form the possessive of a plural noun that ends in s, simply add an apostrophe.
the friends that belong to the girls   the girls' friends

To form the possessive of a plural noun that does not end in s, add an apostrophe and s ('s).
the hopes that belong to the children   the children's hopes

Rewrite each phrase as a possessive.

1. the daughter that belongs to Mommy _____

2. the city that belongs to Zlata _____

3. the birds that belong to the sisters _____

4. the rights that belong to people _____

5. the homework that belongs to the class _____

6. the children that belong to Serbia _____

7. the stories that belong to the women _____

8. the house that belongs to the grandparents _____

9. the worries that belong to a family _____

10. the tears that belong to the men _____

SKILLS FOR WRITING

Use with textbook page 169.

Writing Eyewitness Reports

A good **eyewitness report** answers **wh- questions**, uses **pronouns**, helps readers **visualize**, and includes interesting **details**. Read this excerpt from *Zlata's Diary*. Then answer the questions about the diary entry, or "eyewitness report," using details from it.

Wednesday, May 27, 1992
Dear Mimmy,

SLAUGHTER! MASSACRE! HORROR! CRIME! BLOOD! SCREAMS! TEARS! DESPAIR!

That's what Vaso Miskin Street looks like today. Two shells exploded in the street and one in the market. Mommy was nearby at the time. She ran to Grandma and Granddad's. Daddy and I were beside ourselves because she hadn't come home. I saw some of it on TV but still can't believe what I actually saw. It's unbelievable. I've got a lump in my throat and a knot in my tummy. HORRIBLE! They're taking the wounded to the hospital. It's a madhouse.

1. Write the sentence that answers this question: What happened?

_____

2. Write the words that answer this question: When did it happen?

_____

3. Write the words that answer this question: Where did it happen?

_____

4. Write the words that answer this question: Where was Zlata's mother at the time?

_____

5. Write details that answer this question: Who was involved?

_____

6. Write how you think Zlata would have answered: Why did it happen?

_____

7. Write some details that help readers visualize what happened.

_____

8. Circle details that help you understand how Zlata felt about what happened.

9. Underline all pronouns. Where you can, draw a line to the noun the pronoun replaces.

10. What does the pronoun *it* refer to? _____

PROOFREADING AND EDITING

Use with textbook page 170.

Read this eyewitness report carefully. Look for errors in the use of apostrophes to show possession. Watch for places where a pronoun could be used to replace a noun. There are also errors in capitalization, spelling, and punctuation. Find the mistakes. Then rewrite the eyewitness report correctly on the lines below.

A Peace Treaty for the balkans

Paris, france, december 14, 1995—Todays events in the Balkans were very important, and I was there. The leaders of Bosnia, serbia, and Croatia signed a peace treaty. The leaders of Bosnia, Serbia, and Croatia worked hard to acheive this goal. I was one of the translators assistant.

The crowds mood was very serius. More then 200,000 people have died in the war. A treaty cannot bring more than 200,000 people who have died in the war back to live. Last, the leaders signed the treaty. Then the leaders gave short speeches. Their words encouraged we. The Croatian president called the treaty "a major stride forward.

I hope it is. Unfortunutly, too bombs fell on a Hotel in sarajevo while the treaty being signed.

_____

_____

_____

_____

_____

_____

_____

_____

_____

_____

_____

SPELLING

Use after the spelling lesson.

Adding -es

To form the present tense of regular verbs, add
-s or -es when the subject of the sentence
is singular.

The birds *sing*.	The baby birds *hatch*.
The bird *sings*.	The baby bird *hatches*.

Add -es if the verb ends with the letters -*ch*,
-*sh*, -*s*, -*x*, or -*z*. Notice another spelling change
in the word *quizzes*.

watch ➤ watches   wish ➤ wishes
kiss ➤ kisses   wax ➤ waxes
quiz ➤ quizzes

Complete each sentence. Write the correct present tense form of the verb in
parentheses. (Hint: One subject below is plural, so the verb does not need -s.)

1. Zlata _____ people in her family. (watch)

2. She _____ in her diary. (write)

3. Everyone _____ that the war would end soon. (wish)

4. The young girl _____ her old life. (miss)

5. Zlata's mother _____ her many useful lessons. (teach)

6. An editor _____ Zlata's diary. (read)

7. His company _____ the young writer's diary. (publish)

8. Readers _____ the published diary in many stores. (buy)

9. The diary _____ people understand the war in Sarajevo. (help)

10. Zlata's writing _____ great joy and terrible sadness. (mix)

UNIT 5 We Can Be Heroes

PART 1

Contents

VOCABULARY

Use with textbook page 181.

Complete each sentence. Use the words in the box. You will not use all of the words.

deeds	beliefs	imprisoned	passive resistance
tolerance	protests	symbols	social justice

1. Many people shared her strong _____ and values, but they were afraid to live by them.

2. The hero's actions and brave _____ saved many people from harm.

3. The man was _____ because he had committed a serious crime.

4. The group used nonviolent confrontation and _____ to protest against unfair laws.

5. The new president believed in _____ and treated everyone fairly.

Read the clues. Use the words in the box to complete the crossword puzzle. (Hint: You will not use all the words.)

beliefs	deeds	spent	justice	protected
brave	passive	protest	symbols	tolerance

ACROSS
1. fair treatment
4. not active
5. actions

DOWN
2. willingness to respect others' ideas, customs, or opinions
3. strongly held ideas about something

VOCABULARY BUILDING

Understanding Homophones

Homophones are words that sound the same but have different meanings and different spellings. The words *to, too,* and *two* are homophones. Study these examples.

hour / our	know / no
I'm reading my report in one <u>hour</u>.	Do you <u>know</u> any heroic people?
It's all about <u>our</u> greatest American heroes.	I'm <u>no</u> hero, but I think my dad is!
rights / writes	**plains / planes**
The Constitution gives people equal <u>rights</u>.	Did <u>planes</u> fly in World War I?
The student <u>writes</u> a report about heroes.	Pioneers traveled across the <u>plains</u>.
one / won	**there / their / they're**
The soldiers <u>won</u> the battle for freedom.	<u>There</u> are many unknown heroes.
Only <u>one</u> person spoke about social justice.	<u>Their</u> good deeds will never be known.
	<u>They're</u> not in the news.

Read each sentence and underline the correct homophone.

1. Do you (know / no) _____ the name Benito Juárez?

2. As a young boy, he had little or (know / no) _____ education.

3. He became a lawyer and then (one / won) _____ the election for governor.

4. (One / Won) _____ of his goals was to help the Zapotec people.

5. (They're / There) _____ are many stories about his many reforms.

Circle the incorrect homophone in each sentence. Write the correct word on the line.

Example: Many people were going about (there) day as usual.   *their*

6. Know American was prepared for September 11, 2001.   _____

7. Two plains flew into the Word Trade Center towers.   _____

8. Hour nation was under attack.   _____

9. New Yorkers showed how much they loved there city.   _____

10. The mayor said it was the firefighters' "darkest day and finest our."   _____

READING STRATEGY

Use with textbook page 181.

Making Inferences

When you **make inferences**, you use what an author tells you and what you already know to help you "complete the picture." Here is an example of how to make inferences.

What the author clearly tells you	What you already know	What the author does not clearly tell you, or what you infer
A seventeen-year-old girl led the huge French army in a fight against the English.	Soldiers will only follow a good leader.	The young woman was a great leader to have so many people follow her into battle.

Read the following sentences. Then write what you know about this kind of situation. Finally, write what the writer has not clearly told you, or what you infer.

What the writer clearly tells me	What I already know	What I infer
1. At age thirteen, Benito Juárez could not read, speak, or write Spanish. Later, he became the first Zapotec Indian president of Mexico.		
2. In 1962, Nelson Mandela was arrested and sent to prison for speaking against South Africa's government. In 1994, he became president of South Africa.		
3. Florence Nightingale's parents did not want her to become a nurse. She traveled to Turkey during the Crimean War and helped many wounded soldiers.		
4. For years, Mohandas Gandhi was a leader in India's struggle for independence. In 1948, he was assassinated.		
5. A small group of French doctors started Doctors Without Borders in 1971. The group won the Nobel Peace Prize in 1999.		

Use with textbook pages 190–192.

Summary: "Wind Beneath My Wings," "Sebastião Salgado," and from *Leaves of Grass*

"Wind Beneath My Wings" is a song about how heroes can simply be people who love us. "Sebastião Salgado" tells about the photographer who faces personal danger to take pictures of refugees and other people struggling to survive. Walt Whitman's lines from *Leaves of Grass* describe an injured firefighter bravely waiting to be rescued by other firefighters.

Visual Summary

What Is a Hero?
• "Wind Beneath My Wings": People, seemingly unnoticed, who love and support us from the background
• "Sebastião Salgado": Those who risk danger to show the world what has happened
• from *Leaves of Grass*: Brave firefighters risking their lives to help others and rescue fellow firefighters

Name _____ Date _____

Wind Beneath My Wings

<table>
</table>

Use What You Know

List three of your heroes.

1. _____

2. _____

3. _____

Text Structure: Song

A song is lyrics set to music. Like many poems, most songs have lines grouped together in stanzas of a fixed number of lines. Often they include a chorus, a stanza that is repeated after each one or two other stanzas. Circle the stanza that is a chorus in this song. **MARK THE TEXT** List some words and phrases that are repeated in this song.

_____

_____

Reading Strategy: Making Inferences

Inferences are logical guesses you make by combining the information in a selection with your own knowledge and experience. Underline two details about the singer and two about the person being sung to. What do **MARK THE TEXT** you infer that the singer means by "you are the wind beneath my wings"?

_____

_____

_____

It must have been cold there in my shadow,

To never have sunlight on your face.

You were content to let me shine,

    that's your way.

You always walked a step behind.

So I was the one with all the glory,

While you were the one with all the strain.

A beautiful face without a name for so long.

A beautiful smile to hide the pain.

Chorus

Did you ever know that you're my hero,

And everything I would like to be?

I can fly higher than an eagle,

For you are the wind beneath my wings.

It might have appeared to go unnoticed,

But I've got it all here in my heart.

I want you to know I know the truth,

    of course I know it.

I would be nothing without you.

Fly, fly, fly high against the sky,

So high I almost touch the sky.

Thank you, thank you,

Thank God for you, the wind beneath my wings.

Larry Henley
and
Jeff Silbar

Sebastião Salgado

Sebastião Salgado was once a successful economist. Then, on a trip to Africa in 1973, he decided to become a photographer. For many years he bravely photographed wars and other crises for news agencies. In the 1980s, he worked with Doctors Without Borders in the Sahel region of Africa during a major **drought** and **famine**. Concerned about the millions of refugees, migrants, and dispossessed, Salgado has photographed in thirty-nine countries, such as India, Pakistan, Sudan, Congo, Ethiopia, and Angola. Why? "My photographs . . . give the person who does not have the opportunity to go there the possibility to look. . . ."

Salgado's photographs show people's courage and dignity as they struggle to achieve basic human rights. Today, he is one of the world's most respected photographers. He has published ten books and won many awards.

---

drought, a time when no rain falls and the land becomes very dry
famine, grave shortage of food; starvation

Reading Strategy: Making Inferences

Circle the details that tell when Salgado became a photographer and what he is concerned about. Based on this information, what can you infer is Salgado's main reason for becoming a photographer?

_____

_____

_____

Comprehension Check

Underline the sentence that tells what Salgado bravely photographs. In what way are these actions brave?

_____

_____

_____

Text Structure: Biographical Sketch

A biographical sketch is a short description of another person's life and achievements. Underline the information about Salgado's achievements in the last paragraph. In addition to Salgado, who else does this sketch praise?

_____

_____

from Leaves of Grass

Comprehension Check

Underline details that show what happened to the one fireman and what the others are doing. How would you sum up the situation?

MARK THE TEXT

_____

_____

Reading Strategy: Making Inferences

Circle the sounds that the "mashed" firefighter hears. Based on the details and your own experience, how might the firefighter be feeling?

MARK THE TEXT

_____

_____

Text Structure: Poem

Whitman's poems do not usually have rhymes or stanzas. How would you describe the kinds of lines he uses here? Write your ideas on the lines below.

_____

_____

_____

Instead of rhyme, the poet uses onomatopoeia—that is, he uses words that suggest what the words mean. Read the poem out loud. Underline the example of onomatopoeia two times.

MARK THE TEXT

I am the mashed fireman, with breast-bone
    broken … tumbling walls buried me in their
debris—
Heat and smoke, I respired … I heard the yelling
    shouts of my comrades—
I heard the distant click of their picks and shovels.
They have cleared the beams away… they tenderly
    lift me forth.

                                        Walt Whitman

---

mashed, injured
debris, broken pieces
comrades, fellow workers and friends
beams, long heavy pieces of wood or metal used in building
    houses
tenderly, gently

Choose one and complete it.
1. Draw a picture of a hero or something a hero does.
2. Do research on the Internet to find out more about Doctors Without Borders. Take notes on the information you find.
3. If you were setting the lines from *Leaves of Grass* to music, what sort of music would you use? Describe the music and why it would suit Whitman's poem.

Retell It!

Write a one-paragraph news report based on the lines from *Leaves of Grass*. You can supply details not included in Whitman's lines, such as the names of the firefighters or the building or city where they were working.

_____

_____

_____

_____

_____

_____

_____

Reader's Response

Which of the people in these selections do you find the most heroic? Why?

_____

_____

_____

_____

_____

Think About the Skill

How did making inferences help you better understand these selections?

_____

_____

_____

_____

_____

GRAMMAR

Use with textbook page 194.

Passive Voice
Verbs in sentences are either in the **active voice** or **passive voice**. The **active voice** focuses on the performer of the action.

The **passive voice** focuses on who or what *receives* the action. To form the **passive voice**, use a form of *be* + the past participle of the verb. The phrase *by* + a noun or pronoun tells who or what performed the action.

Read each sentence. Underline the verb. In the space provided, write **A** if the verb is active, and **P** if the verb is passive.

Example: ___*P*___ Florence Nightingale <u>was born</u> into a wealthy English family.

_____ **1.** Girls from wealthy families usually didn't work.

_____ **2.** Florence Nightingale saved the lives of many wounded soldiers.

_____ **3.** She was called "The Lady with the Lamp."

_____ **4.** Benito Juárez was admired by the people of Oaxaca.

_____ **5.** The people elected Juárez as governor of Oaxaca in 1847.

_____ **6.** Every child was given the chance to go to school.

_____ **7.** Mexico became a more modern society.

_____ **8.** Oskar Schindler is honored as a hero.

_____ **9.** These heroes inspire people today.

_____ **10.** Doctors Without Borders provided medical aid to more than eighty countries.

GRAMMAR

Use after the lesson about capitalization.

...talization.

	Examples
	A hero can be young or old. **I**s she a hero?
	Florence **N**ightingale, **N**elson **M**andela
	Mayor **R**udolph **G**iuliani
	Empire **S**tate **B**uilding, **F**rance, **L**ondon
	August, **D**ecember
Capitalize the names of organizations.	**A**frican **N**ational **C**ongress, **D**octors **W**ithout **B**orders
Capitalize the first and important words in titles, such as book, article, or story titles.	*Schindler's List* "**H**eroes: **Y**esterday and **T**oday"

Read the sentences below. Underline every letter that should be capitilized.

1. last may, my friend selma santiago visited new york city.

2. she saw the place where the world trade center once stood.

3. when she came back to san diego, she wrote an article for a newspaper called the *union tribune*.

4. her article, "turning sadness into hope," inspired many people to do positive things for their city.

5. selma won a contest called "local heroes" because she really made a difference in her community.

SKILLS FOR WRITING

Use with textbook page 195.

Using Time Phrases to Write Biographies

Read the **time phrases** in the box above each group of sentences. Then write the phrase that completes each sentence in the space provided. Make sure the sentences show correct chronological order.

Seventeen years later	in 1412	Two years after that

1. Joan of Arc was born _____.

2. _____, she led the French army against English troops.

3. _____, Joan of Arc was captured and executed.

Today	After she arrived in Turkey	In 1854

4. _____, Florence Nightingale volunteered to help wounded soldiers in the Crimean War.

5. _____, she helped wounded soldiers recover from wounds.

6. _____, you can visit Florence Nightingale's school for nurses in England.

at age eighty	Four years after that
In 1962	twenty-eight years later

7. _____, Nelson Mandela was arrested for speaking out against South Africa's government.

8. He was finally released from prison _____.

9. _____, the people of South Africa elected Mandela as their president.

10. Mandela retired _____.

PROOFREADING AND EDITING

Use with textbook page 196.

Read the biography carefully. Find the mistakes. There are errors in passive voice verbs, verb agreement, verb tense, capitalization, spelling, and punctuation. Rewrite the biography correctly on the lines below.

A South American hero

Simon bolivar was a great south American hero. He was a powerful General. He helped many countrys become independent

In 1783. Simon Bolivar were born in Venezuela. At that time, Venezuela ruled by Spain. When he was three, His father dead. Six years after that. his Mother died. His parents left Bolivar money. At age sixteen, he went to spain to be educated.

When Bolivar returned to venezuela, he helped the country fight for independence, In later years, Bolivar helped panama, Colombia Ecuador, and Peru gain independence. Another South American country named in his honor. It is call Bolivia.

_____

_____

_____

_____

_____

_____

_____

_____

_____

_____

_____

_____

_____

SPELLING

Use after the spelling lesson.

Silent Letters: *wr, kn*

Some words have **silent letters**. The letter *w* is silent in words that begin with *wr-*.

   write   wrist

The letter *k* is silent in words that begin with *kn-*.

   knock   knew

Read the sentences below. Choose the correct word in parentheses ( ) to complete the sentence and write it in the space provided.

1. Benito Juárez could not (right / write) _____ Spanish when he was a boy.

2. Juárez believed that every child had the (right / write) _____ to an education.

3. Florence Nightingale (knew / new) _____ she wanted to be a nurse.

4. Nightingale started a (knew / new) _____ school for nurses in England.

5. Nelson Mandela did not (no / know) _____ he would be elected president someday.

Read the words in the box below. Use the words to answer the questions. (Hint: You will not use all the words.)

wrinkle	wren	wreck	wrist	knead	wrath	knob	kneel

6. Which word has silent *k* and rhymes with *wheel*? _____

7. Which word has silent *w* and rhymes with *twist*? _____

8. Which word has silent *k* and rhymes with *bead*? _____

9. Which word has silent *w* and rhymes with *bath*? _____

10. Which word has silent *w* and rhymes with *twinkle*? _____

UNIT 5 We Can Be Heroes

PART 2

Contents

VOCABULARY

Use with textbook page 199.

Complete each sentence. Use the words and phrases in the box. You will not use all of the words.

destination	go into hiding	identity	impression
regulations	invaded	anxious	forbidden

1. One way to make a good first _____ is to smile at people.

2. A favorite _____ for a winter vacation is a ski resort.

3. People have birth certificates and passports to show their _____.

4. Schools have rules and _____ to keep order.

5. In times of war, some people must _____ to be safe from harm.

Read the clues. Use the words in the box to complete the crossword puzzle. (Hint: You will not use all the words.)

carefree	colleagues	destination	exhausted	forbidden
conspicuous	identity	impression	military	regulations

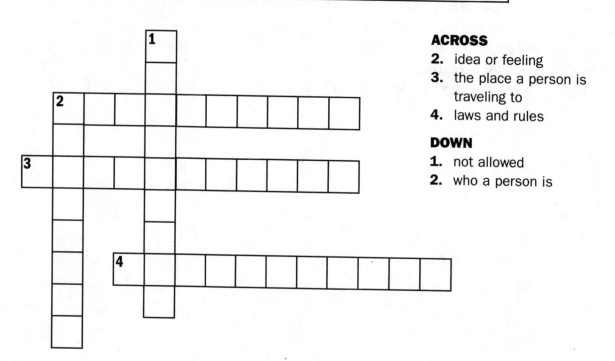

ACROSS
2. idea or feeling
3. the place a person is traveling to
4. laws and rules

DOWN
1. not allowed
2. who a person is

VOCABULARY BUILDING

Using Affixes and Base Words

You can often understand a new word if you know the meaning of its **base**. Some words have a **prefix** (part added at the beginning of the base word) and/or a **suffix** (part added at the end of the base word). You can put together the meaning of the **affix** (the prefix or suffix) + **the base word** to discover the word's meaning.

This chart shows some common affixes.

Prefixes		Suffixes	
il-, in-, un-	not	-er	one who
dis-	opposite of	-ly	in a way; like
re-	again	-ous	full of
		-ful	full of
		-ion	action or process

Read each sentence below. Pay attention to the word in **boldfaced** type. The base part of the word is underlined. Put together the meaning of the base and the affix to figure out the meaning of the word. Write the meaning in the space provided.

1. We left the beds **unmade**. _____

2. This gave the **impression** that we left in a hurry. _____

3. We were afraid because going into hiding was **illegal**. _____

4. Hiding was **dangerous**, but we had no other choice. _____

5. Miep would be our **helper** while we were hiding. _____

6. Peter **solemnly** shook hands with my mother. _____

7. He was worried because his parents **disappeared**. _____

8. He waited **nervously** for them to arrive. _____

9. I was **resentful** that we had to live this way. _____

10. I hoped that someday I could **regain** a normal life. _____

READING STRATEGY

Use with textbook page 199.

Visualizing

Visualizing means making a picture in your mind. In a play, the stage directions help you picture the setting (where the play takes place), the characters' appearances, and their actions. Stage directions are usually in special type and parentheses. Here is an example of stage directions from *The Diary of Anne Frank*.

> (As Mr. Frank pulls a large tarpaulin off the kitchen table, he sees a rat move across the floor. Mrs. Frank shrieks.)

These stage directions help you visualize what happens when Mr. Frank uncovers a rat.

In your textbook, read the last three lines on page 201 and the left column on page 202. Then answer the questions about the stage directions.

1. What does Mrs. Frank do when she sees the rat? What do you picture when you read these stage directions?

   _____

   _____

2. Mr. Frank tells his wife to be quiet. How do you picture him doing this?

   _____

   _____

3. Who appears on the steps? What is he doing? How do you picture him?

   _____

   _____

4. What do you notice about Peter's appearance? Do the stage directions tell you about how he is dressed?

   _____

5. Anne welcomes Peter to the Annex. How does she do this? How do you think she looks when she greets him?

   _____

   _____

Use with textbook pages 208–210.

Summary: "Heroic Art"

Spanish artist Pablo Picasso painted a mural about a town called Guernica that was bombed during the Spanish Civil War in 1937. His painting shows the horror of war. In 1995, Yasuda Tadashi started a world art project in Kyoto, Japan, called Kids' Guernica. He invited children from all over the world to make paintings for peace.

Visual Summary

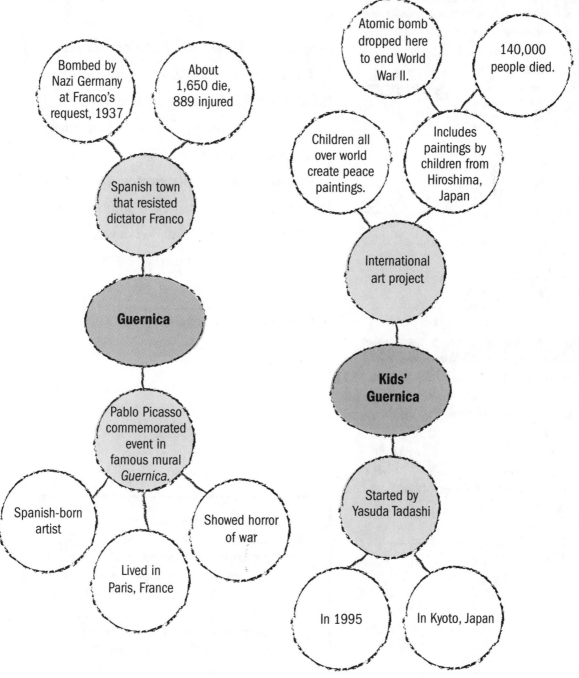

Heroic Art

Guernica

During the Spanish Civil War (1936–1939), Spain was a divided country. A large group of Spaniards hated General Franco, Spain's fascist dictator. This group was called the Resistance. The Resistance wanted to defeat Franco's government, but Franco was a powerful leader. Franco was supported by Hitler (the leader of Nazi Germany) and Mussolini (the leader of fascist Italy). The Resistance made Franco very angry.

At this time, Guernica, a town in northern Spain, had a population of 7,000. Guernica was independent and democratic. On April 26, 1937, Franco ordered Nazi planes to bomb the town. It was 4:00 P.M. on a busy market day. About 1,650 innocent people were killed and 889 injured.

---

dictator, a ruler who has complete power over a country

Choose one and complete it.
1. Draw your own peace painting.
2. Do research on the Internet to find out more about what happened in Guernica in 1937 or Hiroshima in 1945. Take notes on the information you find.
3. Imagine you were viewing the peace paintings for Kids' Guernica. Describe your likely reaction.

Pablo Picasso

Picasso (1881–1973) was one of the most important artists of the twentieth century. He was born in Spain and moved to Paris when he was twenty-three.

After the bombing of Guernica, Picasso was shocked by the black-and-white photographs he saw in the newspapers. He quickly sketched the first images for a mural. *Guernica* shows the horror and chaos of war.

Picasso wrote this prose-poem about the bombing of Guernica.

> . . . *cries of children cries of women cries of birds cries of flowers cries of timbers and of stones cries of bricks cries of furniture of beds of chains of curtains of pots and of papers cries of odor which claw at one another cries of smoke pricking the shoulder of cries . . .*

---

chaos, confusion
prose-poem, descriptive writing that is similar to poetry

Choose one and complete it.
1. Do a fictional interview with Picasso. Use the information above to write questions and answers.
2. Create a drawing using the details from Picasso's prose-poem.
3. Create your own prose-poem or expression of how you feel about the chaos of war.

Comprehension Check

Draw a box around the word that tells how Picasso felt about the newspaper pictures of Guernica. What emotions do you think his painting of Guernica probably conveys?

_____

_____

_____

Text Structure: Informational Text

Underline the information about where Picasso was born. From what you know of his background, why do you think the scenes of Guernica had such a strong impact on him?

_____

_____

_____

Reading Strategy: Visualizing

Circle three details in Picasso's prose-poem that help you visualize the effects of the bombing of Guernica. In addition to the sense of sight, to which senses does the prose-poem appeal?

_____

_____

_____

Comprehension Check

Underline the words that tell you what Kids' Guernica is. Why do you think Yasuda Tadashi decided to associate his project with Picasso's *Guernica*?

_____

_____

_____

_____

Reading Strategy: Visualizing

Circle words that help you picture the kids' paintings. What people, places, or things do you think might appear in the peace paintings?

_____

_____

_____

_____

Text Structure: Informational Text

Underline the information provided about Hiroshima in World War II. What does Hiroshima have in common with the town of Guernica?

_____

_____

_____

_____

Kids' Guernica

Kids' Guernica is an international art project for peace. In 1995, Yasuda Tadashi started the project in Kyoto, Japan. Using the Internet, Tadashi organized schools around the world to participate in the project. His idea was for children in different parts of the world to create peace paintings on huge canvases the same size as Pablo Picasso's *Guernica*. Children participate in workshops in their schools and create their paintings. So far, more than 500 children from schools in Cambodia, Sri Lanka, Chile, Nepal, India, Algeria, Germany, the United States, Australia, China, Canada, France, Italy, and other countries have participated. Their paintings express powerful messages of peace.

In 1945, the United States dropped an **atomic bomb** on the city of Hiroshima, Japan, ending World War II. The city was completely destroyed. In 1999, forty-one students from four elementary schools in Hiroshima participated in the Kids' Guernica project. These schools are all located in the area where the bomb exploded. The students created their mural in memory of the 140,000 people who died and to express their hope for peace in the future.

---

canvases, strong cloths on which artists paint pictures
atomic bomb, a weapon that causes a huge explosion and kills many people

Retell It!

Imagine that students in your area are going to contribute to Kids' Guernica and you are reporting their plans in the school newspaper. Write a very short news article about the project.

_____

_____

_____

_____

_____

_____

Reader's Response

What is your own opinion of the Kids' Guernica project? Why?

_____

_____

_____

_____

_____

Think About the Skill

How did visualizing help you better understand what you read?

_____

_____

_____

_____

_____

_____

GRAMMAR

Use with textbook page 212.

Comparative and Superlative Adjectives

A **comparative adjective** compares two things, and a **superlative adjective** compares three or more things. Remember, some adjectives have irregular comparative and superlative forms.

Write the comparative and superlative forms of each adjective on the charts.

Comparative and Superlative Adjectives of One Syllable

Adjective	Comparative	Superlative
1. hard	_____ than	the _____
2. calm	_____ than	the _____
3. smart	_____ than	the _____

Comparative and Superlative Adjectives of Two or More Syllables

Adjective	Comparative	Superlative
4. nervous	_____ than	the _____
5. dangerous	_____ than	the _____
6. serious	_____ than	the _____
7. fantastic	_____ than	the _____
8. shaken	_____ than	the _____

Two Irregular Comparative and Superlative Adjectives

Adjective	Comparative	Superlative
9. good	_____ than	the _____
10. bad	_____ than	the _____

GRAMMAR

Use after the lesson on comparative adverb forms.

Comparative Adverbs

Comparative adverbs compare two actions. The word *than* is often used after a comparative adverb. Here are three ways to form comparative adverbs.

a. To form the comparative of a one-syllable adverb, add *-er*.	fast hard	Dia paints *faster than* anyone else. He works *harder* today *than* yesterday.
b. To form the comparative of an adverb ending in *-ly*, use *more* or *less*.	brightly hurriedly	Gold glows *more brightly than* silver. Ty paints *less hurriedly than* Andre.
c. To form the comparative of an irregular adverb, change the spelling.	good bad	Some artists painted *better than* others. The blue paint drips *worse than* the green.

Circle the comparative form of the adverb in each sentence. In the space provided, write the letter of the rule above (**a, b,** or **c**) that describes the adverb in the sentence.

_____ **1.** Franco governed more harshly than other Spanish leaders.

_____ **2.** He thought less democratically than many Europeans.

_____ **3.** His tanks and planes moved faster than lightning.

_____ **4.** People in Guernica thought more independently than Franco wanted them to.

_____ **5.** They paid more dearly for their thinking than other cities.

_____ **6.** The children's cries sounded worse than the bombs.

Use each verb and comparative adverb in a sentence.

7. ran slower than _____

8. played worse than _____

9. climbed higher than _____

10. shone more brightly than _____

SKILLS FOR WRITING

Use with textbook page 213.

Writing Reviews

A review is a type of persuasive writing. The writer of a review gives his or her opinion about a book, a play, a movie, or an art exhibit.

Choose the play: *The Diary of Anne Frank* or Picasso's mural *Guernica* to review for your school newspaper. To plan your review, answer the following questions.

1. What work are you reviewing? _____

_____

_____

_____

2. How did you feel about the work? Did you like or dislike it? _____

_____

_____

3. What details can you give to support your feelings? _____

_____

_____

4. What did you learn from the work that you didn't know before? _____

_____

_____

5. Would you recommend this work to friends or classmates? Why? _____

_____

_____

PROOFREADING AND EDITING

Use with textbook page 214.

Read the review carefully. Find the mistakes. There are errors in forming comparative and superlative forms of adjectives and adverbs, spelling, and capitalization. Rewrite the review correctly on the lines below.

A review of the Diary of Anne Frank

I saw our school production of The Dairy of Anne Frank last night. It was the best play I have seen at our school. All the actors performed more professionallyer than the ones in last year's musical. The play tells the most sad story I know. Anne and her family hide from the Nazis in a small section of a building.

The set was one of the most strongest parts of the play. The lighting was more dark than normal. The costumes were also more gray than cloths in real life. The acting was the best part of the evening. The student playing Anne gave the most heartbreaking preformance. She is one of the most talented actors in are school.

Go see this play. It is more powerful acted than I expected.

_____

_____

_____

_____

_____

_____

_____

_____

_____

_____

_____

_____

_____

SPELLING

Use after the spelling lesson.

Changing y to i to Add -er and -est

To form a comparative of words that end in *y*, change the *y* to *i* and add *-er*.

   happy + *-er* = happier   funny + *-er* = funnier

To form a superlative of words that end in *y*, change the *y* to *i* and add *-est*.

   happy + *-est* = happiest   funny + *-er* = funniest

Complete the chart. Spell the words correctly.

Word	Comparative (+ -er)	Superlative (+ -est)
1. early		
2. friendly		
3. busy		
4.	easier	
5.		fuzziest

Read each sentence. Write the comparative or the superlative form of the word below the line.

1. (superlative) That is the _____ painting I have ever seen!
                         ugly

2. (comparative) I think that painting is _____ than drawing.
                              tricky

3. (comparative) My art class is _____ than my math class.
                        easy

4. (superlative) That mural is the _____ art in our school.
                        funny

5. (comparative) Red is a _____ color than gray.
                    lively

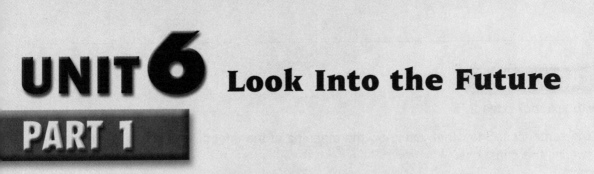

UNIT 6 Look Into the Future

PART 1

Contents

VOCABULARY

Use with textbook page 225.

Read the sentences. Show that you know the meaning of the underlined word or words by answering the questions.

1. When new inventions are <u>mass-produced</u>, they cost less. What do you own that was

   <u>mass-produced</u>? _____

2. <u>Traffic jams</u> make people late to school and work. Where might there be <u>traffic jams</u>

   near you? _____

3. We have explored most <u>frontiers</u> on this planet. Where do you think the next

   <u>frontiers</u> may be? _____

4. <u>Robots</u> may soon fight fires. How will using <u>robots</u> instead of people make fire

   fighting safer? _____

5. The population has grown so fast that there are six times more people now than in

   the 1800s. Why do you think the <u>population</u> has grown so fast? _____

   _____

Read the clues. Use the words in the box to complete the crossword puzzle. (Hint: You will not use all the words.)

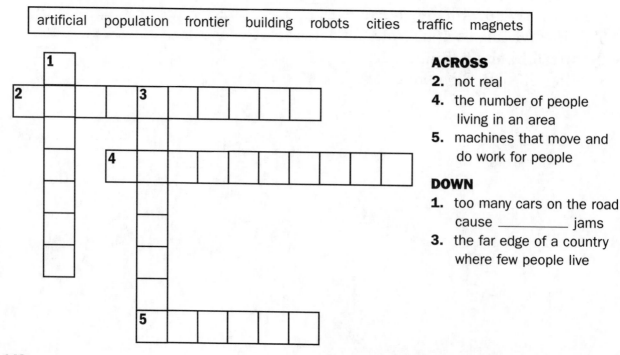

artificial   population   frontier   building   robots   cities   traffic   magnets

ACROSS
2. not real
4. the number of people living in an area
5. machines that move and do work for people

DOWN
1. too many cars on the road cause _____ jams
3. the far edge of a country where few people live

VOCABULARY BUILDING

Using Print and Online Resources to Find Spelling and Meaning

You can use a dictionary to find the spelling or meaning of a word. Remember these tips when you use a print dictionary:

- Words in a dictionary are arranged in alphabetical order.
- Nouns are listed in their singular form.
- Verbs are listed in the base form, such as *fly, explore,* or *invent.* So if you want to know about the verb *buried*, you would look up *bury.*

A dictionary entry has different kinds of information. Read the following entries:

> **progress** (PROG res) n. **1.** a forward movement **2.** development or improvement
> **progress** (pro GRES) v. **1.** to move forward **2.** to improve
> **prohibit** (pro HIB it) v. to not allow; forbid

Read these sentences below. Circle *True* or *False* for each sentence.

1. The word *progress* can be a noun or a verb.   **True**   **False**

2. The word *prohibit* has four syllables.   **True**   **False**

3. The word *prohibit* is the opposite of allow.   **True**   **False**

4. The verb *progress* can mean "a forward movement."   **True**   **False**

5. The noun *progress* can mean "improvement."   **True**   **False**

Online dictionaries can help you find spellings and meanings, too. Look up an online dictionary. On the Web page, type the word you want to find. Click once, and the meaning and spelling will appear. If the dictionary doesn't find the word, try another spelling.

Use a print or online dictionary to find definitions of these words. Write the definition in the space provided.

6. satellite _____

7. launch _____

8. orbit _____

9. prototype _____

10. atmosphere _____

READING STRATEGY

Use with textbook page 225.

Summarizing

Summarizing is retelling the main ideas of a text. A summary is always shorter than the text. It can help you remember important information.

Before you summarize, ask yourself these questions:
- What happened?
- What are the main ideas?

Use some words from the text and some of your own words when you write a summary.

1. Read "The Growing World" on page 227 in your textbook. Circle the letter of the sentence that best summarizes the text.

   a. Population is the number of people living within a given area.

   b. In 1800, the world's population was about one billion.

   c. Because of better health and living conditions, the population on Earth is growing rapidly.

   d. One reason for fast growth is that the birth rate is higher than the death rate.

2. Explain why your choice is the best summary.

   _____

   _____

3. Read "Future Cities" on page 227 in your textbook. Circle the letter of the sentence that best summarizes the text.

   a. In the future, everyone will live in outer space.

   b. Tokyo will be the largest city on Earth.

   c. Cities will be very crowded in the future.

   d. In the future, many people will live in giant buildings that will be like small cities.

4. Explain why your choice is the best summary.

   _____

   _____

5. Read both sections on page 227 in your textbook again, and write a short summary of each.

   _____

   _____

   _____

Use with textbook pages 234–236.

Summary: "Interview with an Astronaut: Dan Bursch"

Dan Bursch is an American astronaut. In this interview, students used the Internet to ask him questions about being an astronaut. Bursch tells about his job on the space station and describes what it feels like to fly into space.

Visual Summary

Who?	Dan Bursch, astronaut
What?	lived in space
When?	December 5, 2001, to June 19, 2002
Where?	International Space Station
Why?	to learn to live and work in space, conduct experiments, and get two former enemies, the U.S. and Russia, working together on an important project
How?	work in zero gravity; divide work up among crew

Name _____   Date _____

Interview with an Astronaut: Dan Bursch

Dan Bursch has made three space flights and has been in space for 746 hours. He lived on the International Space Station from December 5, 2001, until June 19, 2002. Before this expedition, he chatted *with some students on www.discovery.com.*

Dan Bursch: I would just like to say welcome to everyone tonight. Thank you for spending your Sunday evening with me. . . .

Cody: I am ten years old, and I would like to know what the food is like. I would also like for you to trade me just one day in the space station and you can go to my school.

Dan Bursch: Well, thanks, Cody. Food is very important for us up in space, as it is here on Earth. In fact, one of the things that I will be starting tomorrow . . . is food tasting. We are selecting our menu for the four- to six-month flight that I will have in space. What is different about my next mission on the space station is that we will have a mixture of American and Russian food, so that will certainly make it different. . . . Perhaps I can come to your school someday and perhaps in fifteen years or so you can go to space!

Gary TX: What kind of work do you do when you are at the space station?

Dan Bursch: We have a crew of three—myself, Carl Waltz (another American astronaut), and Yuri. He is a Russian cosmonaut. He will be our commander. We divide up the work because there is a lot of work to be done. . . .

Galileo Guest: How do the astronauts deal with the effects of zero gravity on the space station?

Dan Bursch: Learning to work in space without feeling gravity is always a challenge. . . . Getting used to not feeling gravity usually takes a day or two.

---

chatted, talked informally
selecting, choosing
cosmonaut, Russian astronaut
commander, leader

International: What is it like working with scientists and other astronauts from all around the world? Do you all get along? Do you have fun?

Dan Bursch: This job is particularly interesting just because of that fact. . . . In the astronaut office, the range of different kinds of people is pretty wide. . . . But we all share one common goal and that is to fly and live and work in space. . . .

Hollifeld: Can you see the lights of the world's cities from space?

Dan Bursch: Yes. We spend half of our time while in orbit on the dark side of the planet. If there is a thin cloud layer, you see kind of a glow like from a lampshade that dampens the light a little bit. But when it is clear—when there are no clouds—the lights are spectacular. . . .

Venus: What is the first time you go into space like? Is it hard to learn to use the tools or get used to things floating around?

Dan Bursch: I remember my first flight in 1993 on *Discovery*. . . . At lift-off, there is a lot of vibration and a lot of noise, and eight and a half minutes later you are in orbit. When the engines turn off, instantly everything floats. . . . You have to make sure that you either strap something down or use Velcro because you will probably lose it otherwise.

Fun 2 Travl: What are the entertainment options available to you during your down time on the space station?

Dan Bursch: We will have movies that we will be able to play in orbit. . . . People will try to bring up a hobby such as reading. . . . We do have e-mail. Most of our down time will be spent sending e-mails to our families and friends.

---

get along, act friendly
in orbit, circling around Earth
spectacular, wonderful and exciting
floating around, moving around freely in the air
Velcro, a material made of two special pieces of cloth, used for fastening clothes, shoes, etc.
entertainment options, things to do for fun
down time, free time
hobby, something people do for pleasure during free time

Comprehension Check

Based on Dan Bursch's answer to Galileo Guest's question on page 146, how would you define the term "zero gravity"?

_____

_____

_____

Which other interviewer also asks about zero gravity? Circle that question.

Reading Strategy: Summarizing

Underline the main details in Dan Bursch's answer to International's question. Summarize Bursch's answer in one sentence.

_____

_____

_____

Comprehension Check

Underline the key points in Bursch's response to Hollifeld's question. Explain what spending half the time on the dark side of Earth has to do with Hollifeld's question.

_____

_____

_____

_____

Name _____ Date _____

Circle two details about the personal items that astronauts take into space, which Jurgen asks about in his question. Why do you think someone in space would take these sorts of items along for the trip?

_____

_____

_____

_____

_____

Text Structure: Interview

People posting on the Internet often make up special names for themselves. Underline one such name of a student interviewer on this page. Then explain how that name relates to the subject of the interview or the question the interviewer asks.

_____

_____

_____

_____

_____

_____

Jurgen: What kind of personal items will you take with you from Earth?

Dan Bursch: The most popular personal item is probably pictures of our families. Other things may include perhaps a special memento, either from a parent or a grandparent. But the most popular personal items are pictures. And usually ones that include some scene or the background of what it is like back on Earth.

AstroBob: Do you think that at some point ordinary people will get to go to the space station? Or will it always be reserved for scientists?

Dan Bursch: I think that is certainly a goal that we should try to reach. If it will be in my lifetime, I don't know. . . . When airplanes first came out, they were reserved at first for just the very daring or risk takers. And now anybody can fly on an airplane. So, I don't think it is a question of IF the opportunity will come . . . it is simply a matter of WHEN.

Sandy Fay: What kinds of things do they hope the space station will be good for once it is completed?

Dan Bursch: . . . I see the biggest challenge and the biggest thing that we are learning is two former enemies learning how to work together and build such a large and complex structure in space. And not just two former enemies, but all of the over one dozen countries that are working together. . . .

Discovery.com: Thank you, Dan, for chatting with us tonight.

---

memento, an item that helps
    you remember something or
    someone
reserved for, set aside for
daring, brave
complex, not simple; complicated

Retell It!

Imagine you are adapting Dan Bursch's experiences into a TV or film documentary. What details from his interview would you include? List your ideas.

_____

_____

_____

_____

_____

_____

_____

_____

Reader's Response

What would you have taken along if you spent six months in space? Why?

_____

_____

_____

_____

_____

_____

Think About the Skill

How did summarizing help you better understand the selection?

_____

_____

_____

_____

Name _____ Date _____

GRAMMAR

Use with textbook page 238.

Using *will* for the Future
Use ***will* + base form of the verb** to make predictions about the future.
Example: People ***will live*** in giant apartment buildings.

In informal usage, ***will*** is often used to form a contraction. Informal writing includes conversations and dialogue.

- With personal pronouns, an apostrophe is substituted for the letters *wi* in *will*:
Gabriel exclaimed, *"You'll* be surprised. *I'll* fly to the moon!"

- With the word *not, wo* is used and an apostrophe is substituted for the letter *o* in *not*. The contraction for *will not* is *won't*:
She sneezed and sighed, "Just think, on Mars there *won't* be any weeds."

Write a prediction about the future for each topic listed below.
Use **will + base form of a verb**.

Example: food *People will eat only vegetables.*

1. airplanes _____

2. vacations _____

3. robots _____

4. computers _____

5. sports _____

Read the informal sentences. Write the words in parentheses ( ) as a contraction.

6. I'm glad we (will not) _____ be crowded on Mars.

7. (You will) _____ be able to explore new places.

8. (We will) _____ have lots of room to ride our bikes.

9. (We will) _____ probably wear them out fast!

10. But I probably (will not) _____ get a new one, even on Mars!

150

Unit 6 Look into the Future Part 1

GRAMMAR

Use after the lesson about word order in questions.

Word Order in Questions
Questions usually have a helping verb, followed by a subject and a main verb. Questions often begin with question words, such as *who, what, where, when, why,* or *how.*

Question word +	helping verb +	subject +	main verb +	rest of sentence
What	will	people	do	in the future?
When	will	people	drive	flying cars?

Arrange the words to write a question. Begin each question with a question word (*who, what, where, when, why,* or *how*).

1. is   space   what

_____

2. will   Mars   live   people   when   on

_____

3. find   where   you   food   can   artificial

_____

4. do   in   astronauts   how   breathe   space

_____

5. teaches   about   who   astronauts   flying

_____

6. why   robots   popular   are

_____

Write a question (Q) for each answer (A). Use the words in parentheses in your question.

7. Q: _____
A: Leonardo da Vinci (designed flying machines in the 1400s)

8. Q: _____
A: Into the Opening Ceremony of the 1984 summer Olympics ("a rocket man" flew into)

9. Q: _____
A: The SoloTrek Exo-Skeletor Flying Vehicle (the most successful jetpack prototype)

10. Q: _____
A: Jetpacks can fly only a short time. (not used much today)

SKILLS FOR WRITING

Use with textbook page 239.

Writing Notes for a Research Report

Read the rules for taking notes on page 239 in your textbook. Imagine that you are writing a research report about planes of the future and your textbook is a reference source. Reread the section on hypersonic planes on page 229. Then complete these two note cards. Follow these steps:

- Summarize facts that tell about the subtopic. Use some words from the text and some of your own words. For the first note card, use the hints in parentheses. For the second, take notes on important details.
- Note the source: List the title of your textbook, the authors, publisher, place and date of publication, and page number.

Subtopic: Development of the hypersonic plane

1. _____
   (Who's doing what?)

2. _____
   (What will it do?)

3. _____
   (current)

4. _____
   (future)

5. Source: _____
   (title of your textbook, authors, publisher, place and date of publication, and page number)

Subtopic: X-43A prototype plane

6. _____

7. _____

8. _____

9. _____

10. Source: _____

PROOFREADING AND EDITING

Use with textbook page 240.

Read the student newspaper article carefully. Find the mistakes in contractions, punctuation, capitalization, spelling, and word order. Rewrite the article correctly on the lines below.

Will what happen in the Future? Ill let you in on my top ten predictions. If youll answer my question at the end I would appreciate the feedback.

1. People will live in underwater citys.

2. Students will fly to school in plaines.

3. Dog's will grow as large as horses.

4. most houses will had glass floors.

5. Astronauts will explore Saturns rings.

6. Doctors will inserted computer chips in patients

7. football players will wearing shiny metal uniforms.

8. Sientists will discover water on jupiter.

9. Creatures will arrives from other Planets.

10. Robots fight humans.

Now, fellow students, I'm asking you, you do agree? Give me your feedback.

_____

_____

_____

_____

_____

_____

_____

_____

_____

_____

_____

SPELLING

Use after the spelling lesson.

Spelling Diphthong Sounds

This chart shows examples of common spelling patterns for three diphthongs.

/ü/	/ou/	/oi/
school	south	soil
crew	now	toy

Sort these words by their spelling pattern. Write them in the correct space in the chart above.

1. food	**5.** noise	**9.** down	**13.** point
2. around	**6.** joy	**10.** cloud	**14.** soon
3. afternoon	**7.** without	**11.** out	**15.** flew
4. tools	**8.** new	**12.** somehow	**16.** drew

Write four sentences using words from the chart.

17. _____

18. _____

19. _____

20. _____

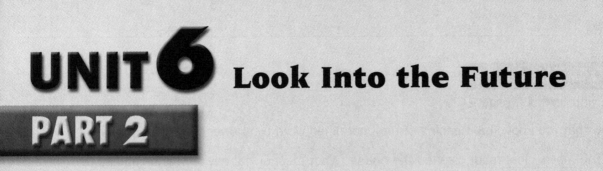

UNIT 6 Look Into the Future

PART 2

Contents

VOCABULARY

Use with textbook page 243.

Show that you know the meaning of the underlined word by answering the questions.

1. The mechanical robot cleaned the house. What mechanical device would you like to

invent to help you? _____

2. Some buildings are more than 100 stories tall. How many stories is the tallest

building you've been in? _____

3. The new high-speed train is very streamlined. How is the new train different from

older trains? _____

4. Revolutionary inventions change the way people live. What is one revolutionary

invention you know about? _____

5. The passengers were transported by a train from one airline to another. In what

other ways are people transported from one place to another? _____

_____

Read the clues. Use the words in the box to complete the crossword puzzle. (Hint: You will not use all the words.)

| antigravity   amazing   streamlined   plastic   revolutionary   stories   transported |

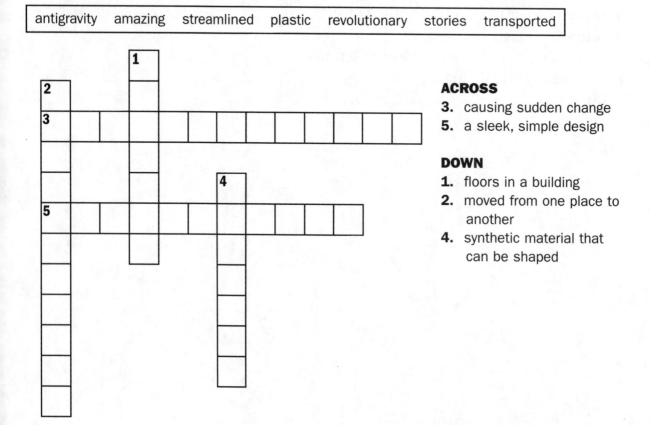

ACROSS
3. causing sudden change
5. a sleek, simple design

DOWN
1. floors in a building
2. moved from one place to another
4. synthetic material that can be shaped

VOCABULARY BUILDING

Understanding Word Origins

It's fun to be a "word detective" and discover where words we use today came from. You can find the origins of words in a dictionary. You may make some interesting discoveries like these:

robot: comes from the Czech word for "work."

museum: comes from the Latin word for "place for learned occupation."

future: comes from the Latin word for "about to be."

past: comes from the Middle English word for "to pass."

disk: comes from the Old English word for "plate."

In the selection you are going to read, three young people visit a <u>museum</u> and find themselves being chased by a <u>robot</u> of the <u>future</u> and dodging people flying around on antigravity <u>disks</u>. To help them get back to their lives in the <u>past</u>, their Uncle Joe finds his pocket watch. Using this context and the meanings given above, as well as a dictionary, define each word. What clues did the word origins give you?

1. **robot** _____

   Clue: _____

   _____

2. **museum** _____

   Clue: _____

   _____

3. **future** _____

   Clue: _____

   _____

4. **past** _____

   Clue: _____

   _____

5. **disk** _____

   Clue: _____

   _____

READING STRATEGY

Use with textbook page 243.

Reading for Enjoyment

When you read, it helps to set a purpose for reading. Ask yourself if you will read to find out information or to be entertained. Reading the title, skimming the text, and looking at the illustrations can help you set a purpose. Answer these questions to help you set a purpose for reading the next selection.

1. From reading the title on page 244 in your textbook, when does the story take place?

   _____

   _____

   _____

2. Will the selection give information about this period of time? Why?

   _____

   _____

3. Look at the illustrations. From the illustrations, what do you think a time warp is?

   _____

   _____

4. What is your purpose for reading this selection—to be informed or to be entertained?

   _____

   _____

5. What do you think the selection will be about?

   _____

   _____

Use with textbook pages 252–254.

Summary: "DNA, Genes, and Traits"

This passage tells about DNA, a special code found in the cells of all living things. Genes inside the DNA control people's traits—the way they look and grow. No two people have the same DNA unless they are identical twins. Scientists use DNA to solve crimes. Tests help them link DNA found at a crime scene with the person who did the crime.

Visual Summary

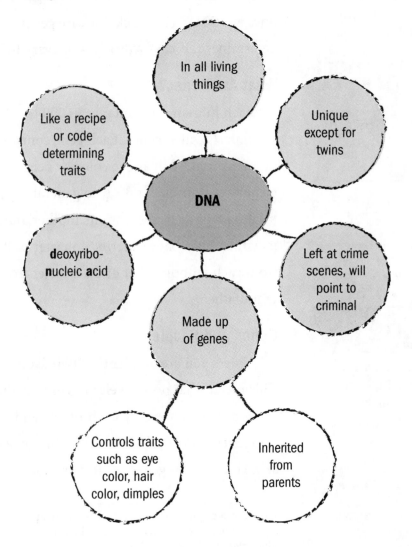

DNA, Genes, and Traits

What is DNA?

Every form of life is put together and controlled by a chemical "recipe," or code, called DNA (deoxyribonucleic acid). DNA is found in cells— very small parts of humans, animals, and plants. DNA contains genes. Genes on DNA look something like a supermarket bar code. The white lines are DNA. The black lines are genes. The code determines the characteristics of every living thing.

What Are Genes?

Each human cell contains 50,000 to 100,000 small parts called genes. Each gene controls a different trait, such as eye color or height. Genes get passed on from generation to generation. A baby inherits half its genes from its mother and half from its father. So, a baby inherits a quarter of its genes from each grandmother and a quarter from each grandfather.

Genes and People

Unless you are an identical twin, you are unique. This means that nobody else has exactly the same genes as you, not even your brothers and sisters.

Genes control all your traits. One gene controls skin color. Three genes control eye color.

---

bar code, a group of thin and thick lines on a product, which a
    computer in a store reads to find the price
characteristics, traits; qualities
generation, all the people who are about the same age in a family
inherits, gets; receives

How Traits Are Inherited

Children often look like their parents in some ways. They can also look like their aunts or uncles, their grandparents, and their great-grandparents. The following traits are often inherited:

- eye color
- hair color
- dimples
- widow's peak
- cleft chin

Dimples are small hollows in the skin. Some people get them around their mouth when they smile. A cleft chin is a dimple in the chin. A hairline that comes to a point in the middle of your forehead is called a widow's peak.

Choose one and complete it.
1. Use the Internet to find a picture of DNA. Then draw a rough sketch of it.
2. Do research at the library or on the Internet to learn how scientists discovered DNA. Take notes on the information you find.
3. Imagine a story that uses DNA testing as part of the plot. Describe your story idea and how DNA testing plays a part in it.

Comprehension Check

Underline five kinds of relatives mentioned in the first paragraph. Why do children often look like these relatives?

_____

_____

_____

Text Structure: Science Article

Science articles often present information in lists or on charts. Circle the list of details on this page. What does it list?

_____

Reading Strategy: Asking Questions

Ask and answer two questions about the information on this page. Write your questions and answers on the lines below.

_____

_____

_____

_____

_____

_____

_____

_____

_____

_____

Reading Strategy: Asking Questions

What question could you ask about the information in the first sentence? Write a question and then answer it on the lines below.

Question: _____

_____

_____

Answer: _____

_____

_____

Comprehension Check

Underline how DNA has affected many prisoners in recent **MARK THE TEXT** years. Why does a match between the DNA at the crime scene and the suspect's DNA show so clearly whether or not the person committed the crime? Write your answer below.

_____

_____

_____

_____

_____

Comprehension Check

Circle the reason that DNA testing will be more important in the future.  **MARK THE TEXT**

DNA and Solving Crimes

Forensic scientists are people who study crimes by looking at **evidence**. Many forensic scientists use scientific or medical tests to solve crimes. One test is for DNA. A sample of blood, hair, or other body **tissue** found at the scene of a crime is tested. The DNA from the sample can be matched to a suspect's DNA to find out if he or she **committed the crime**.

In recent years, many people have been released from prison after DNA tests proved that they were **innocent**. Law students at the Wisconsin Innocence Project **investigate** about twenty to thirty criminal cases at any given time. In 2001, the project was responsible for the release of a Texas prisoner, Chris Ochoa. He was serving a life sentence for a 1988 murder. DNA tests on samples found on the victim proved that Ochoa did not commit the crime. He was innocent. Chris Ochoa spent twelve years in prison for a crime he didn't commit.

DNA testing is now a very important tool in criminal investigation, and it is going to be more important in the future. More forensic scientists are going to use DNA tests to help make sure the right people are punished for their crimes.

---

evidence, proof
tissue, material from the body, such as skin and muscle
committed the crime, did something wrong or illegal
innocent, not guilty
investigate, look into; research

Name _____ Date _____

Write a short newspaper article about Chris Ochoa. Tell what happened to him and how
DNA testing helped him. Also explain what DNA is.

_____

_____

_____

_____

_____

_____

_____

Reader's Response

What do you think of the use of DNA in solving crimes? Explain your views.

_____

_____

_____

_____

_____

_____

_____

Think About the Skill

How did asking questions help you better understand the selection?

_____

_____

_____

_____

_____

Name _____ Date _____

GRAMMAR

Use with textbook page 256.

Using *be going to* for the Future

Read the following sentences about what might happen next in *The Time Warp Trio: 2095*. Cross out *will* in each sentence. Write the correct form of *be* (*am, is, are*) + *going to* in the space provided.

1. They will _____ get The Book back to the past.

2. Then their relatives will _____ have it in 2095.

3. Uncle Joe will _____ use his Time Warp Watch to save the day.

4. The Time Warp Trio will _____ get back to the past.

5. When the three get back, they will _____ write the note about meeting in the Museum of Natural History.

Imagine that the Time Warp Trio is back and can tell friends about what it will be like in the future. Again, cross out *will* in each sentence. Write the correct form of *be* (*am, is, are*) + *going to* in the space provided.

6. People in the future will _____ figure out how to fly.

7. I will _____ discover that a chemical called BHT can make things fly.

8. People will _____ use antigravity disks to fly.

9. People will _____ eat food called Vitagorp.

10. Security guards will _____ be robots.

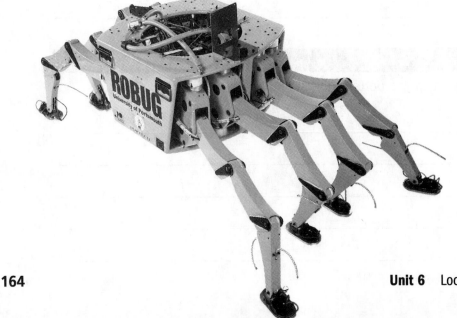

GRAMMAR

Use after the lesson about commas.

Punctuation: Comma

Use a **comma**:

    a. in a compound sentence before the conjunction:
       The friends arrived, and SellBot was waiting for them.

    b. in a series or list: *The SellBot chased Sam, Fred, and Joe.*

    c. after an interjection: *"Hey, you're right!"*

    d. in dialogue to separate the spoken words from the part of the sentence that tells
       who is speaking: *"Look closely," said Sam.*

Add commas to punctuate each sentence below correctly.

   1. A tidal wave of people came in and we were right in its path.

   2. They had corkscrew spike and Mohawk hair in every color you can think of.

   3. "Wow I see it but I don't believe it" said Fred.

   4. There were people with green skin blue skin purple skin orange striped plaid
      dotted and you-name-it skin.

   5. Fred Sam and I looked up and up and up at the building that disappeared in the
      clouds.

   6. "Here's my house" said the lead girl.

   7. The girls catch up and Joe is surprised to see something.

   8. "I got it from my mom" said Samantha.

   9. We copied the girls and Fred ate a handful of the green dog food.

  10. "Hey wait a minute" I said.

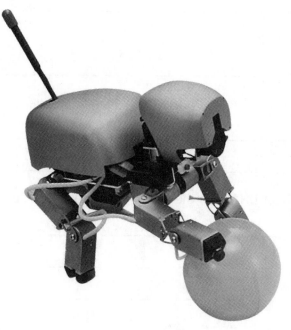

SKILLS FOR WRITING

Use with textbook page 257.

Making Sentence Outlines

Read the outline of the article "DNA, Genes, and Traits" below. Then answer the questions about it.

I. Every form of life is put together and controlled by DNA.
    A. DNA is found in cells.
    B. DNA contains genes.
    C. DNA determines the characteristics of every living thing.
II. Most people are unique and have unique genes.
    A. Only identical twins share the same genes.
    B. Even relatives do not have exactly the same genes.
    C. Genes control skin color and eye color.
III. Traits are inherited.
    A. Some traits are inherited from parents.
    B. Children can look like their relatives.
IV. DNA can be used to find out who committed a crime.
    A. Samples of DNA are tested for a match.
    B. Prisoners have been released based on DNA samples.

1. What is the first main idea?

_____

2. What three details support it?

_____

_____

3. What is the second main idea?

_____

4. What details support the third main idea?

_____

_____

5. What do you find out about DNA from the fourth main idea and supporting details?

_____

_____

_____

PROOFREADING AND EDITING

Use with textbook page 258.

Read the sentence outline carefully. Every main idea and supporting detail should be a complete sentence. Look for errors in the use of *be + going to*, commas, spelling, and capitalization. Rewrite the outline correctly on the lines below.

Humans on Mars

I. Mars will going to have a human city.
  A. Because it is closer than the other planets it will be the first.
  B. People from the US Japan and other countries will travel there.
  C. People going to live in domed cities.

II. Life on Mars are going to be difficult.
  A. Their is no oxygen there.
  B. The environment is cold rocky and dry.
  C. Dust storms cover the whole planet.

III. mars is very different from Earth
  A. The average tempeture on Mars is –81°F
  B. A year on Mars will last 687 Earth days.
  C. To moons orbit Mars.

_____

I. _____

_____

_____

_____

II. _____

_____

_____

_____

III. _____

_____

_____

_____

Name ______________________________ Date ______________

SPELLING

Use after the spelling lesson.

Schwa

Read the two- and three-syllable words below. Listen for the schwa sound in the unaccented syllable or syllables. Write the vowel letter that stands for a schwa sound in the word. If there is more than one schwa sound, write the two letters. If there is no schwa sound, write "none."

_______ **1.** children

_______ **2.** mother

_______ **3.** about

_______ **4.** parent

_______ **5.** widow

_______ **6.** release

_______ **7.** commit

_______ **8.** prison

_______ **9.** travel

_______ **10.** family

ACKNOWLEDGMENTS

Carol Mann Agency. "He Was the Same Age as My Sister" by Mieke C. Malandra, from *I Thought My Father Was God, and Other True Tales,* from NPR's National Story Project, edited and introduced by Paul Auster, 2001. Reprinted by permission of The Carol Mann Agency.

Cinco Puntos Press. "Why Rattlesnake Has Fangs" by Cheryl Giff from *And It Is Still That Way,* collected by Byrd Baylor. Copyright © 1998. Reprinted by permission of Cinco Puntos Press.

Discovery Communications, Inc. "Interview with an Astronaut: Dan Bursch." Copyright © 2000 Discovery Communications, Inc. All rights reserved. www.discovery.com. Reprinted by permission of Discovery Communications, Inc.

Harcourt, Inc. "Grass," from *The Complete Poems of Carl Sandburg.* Copyright © 1970, 1969 by Lilian Steichen Sandburg, Trustee. Reprinted by permission of Harcourt, Inc.

HarperCollins Publishers. "Stolen Rope," "The Cookie Jar," and "School Days," from *More True Lies* by George Shannon. Copyright © 1991 by George W. B. Shannon. Used by permission of HarperCollins Publishers.

Warner Bros. Publications U.S., Inc. "The Wind Beneath My Wings" by Larry Henley and Jeff Silbar. Copyright © 1982 Warner House of Music and WB Gold Music Corp. All rights reserved. Used by permission of Warner Bros. Publications U.S., Inc., Miami, FL 33014.